THE BEDSIDE BOOK OF
GREAT SEXUAL DISASTERS

'And *I* cannot tell a lie either, Mr Washington. In bed,
you're terrible.'

THE BEDSIDE BOOK OF

GREAT SEXUAL DISASTERS

Gyles Brandreth

Illustrated by Michael ffolkes

GRAFTON BOOKS
A Division of the Collins Publishing Group

LONDON GLASGOW
TORONTO SYDNEY AUCKLAND

Grafton Books
A Division of the Collins Publishing Group
8 Grafton Street, London W1X 3LA

Published by Grafton Books 1985

First published in Great Britain
under the title *The Bedside Book of
Great Sexual Disasters* by
Granada Publishing 1984

Copyright © Victorama 1984

ISBN 0-586-06123-1

Made and printed in Great Britain
by Robert Hartnoll (1985) Ltd., Bodmin, Cornwall

CONTENTS

PART 1
Setting the Scene

SEX –
AND BANANA SKINS

'If two people love each other there can
be no happy end to it.'

Ernest Hemingway

'I bet you're a bogus *clergyman* too!'

Sex has been part of my life for as long as I can remember. Even on my birthday, thirty-six years ago, you would have found me naked in bed with an older woman. I like sex and I hope you do too because that's what this book is all about: sex – and banana skins.

Most of us are familiar with sexual disasters: they are what happen to us when we are too young, too old, or too inebriated to know better, and as experiences go they tend to be too personal and too painful to be funny. *Great* sexual disasters, on the other hand, are what happen to other people, and because our personal vanities aren't involved they can be *hilarious*. Inevitably they come in all shapes and sizes – as the actress said to the bish ... no, no, there'll be none of that, I promise – and beset people in every walk of life. They are no respecters of persons, though my researches do suggest that clergymen, doctors and politicians are particularly prone.

It may be that the lives of the clergy seem to be so frequently overwhelmed by sexual mishaps simply because the peccadilloes of the priesthood are more newsworthy than those of, say, authors or chimney sweeps. There are more of them too – and they've been at it longer.

While in this century alone at least three cardinals have suffered the indignity of dying in brothels, Pope Leo VIII is the only pontiff known to have died on the job. His predecessor, John XII, seduced so many women that he was accused of turning St John Lantern into a bordello, and when Balthasar Cossa stepped into the shoes of the fisherman in 1417 his pontificate proved an unmitigated sexual disaster for the women in the neighbourhood. I have it on the best authority, 'Two hundred maids, matrons, and widows, including a few nuns, fell victims to his brutal lust.'

Perhaps the most shameless of St Peter's successors was Roderigo Borgia, father of Cesare and Lucrezia, and known in Rome as Alexander VI. As Pope he enjoyed a succession of mistresses and gave some of the liveliest parties in the history of the church. The Bishop of Ostia recalled a particularly spectacular papal banquet at which 'fifty reputable whores, not common but the kind called courtesans, supped ... and after supper they danced about with the servants and others in the place, first in their clothes and then nude ... candelabra with lighted candles were set on the floor and chestnuts were strewn about and naked courtesans on hands and feet gathered them up, wriggling in and out among the candelabra. ... Then all those present in the hall were carnally treated in public ...' after which the Pope gave prizes to the best performers.

Of course Roderigo Borgia's papacy was as much a spiritual disaster as a sexual one, and it was all a long, long time ago. Contemporary sexual disasters among the clergy tend to be on a more modest level and involve the parish priest rather than the See of Rome. In the newspaper libraries where I have been closeted in recent months I have come across countless tales of local vicars who have left their wives to run off with the lady organist, or the woman who does the flowers, or the cub mistress, or, in two instances, to 'come out' with the curate. I even encountered a report of a wedding that went disastrously wrong when the officiating clergyman got to the line, 'If any know just cause or impediment why these two should not lawfully be joined together let them speak now' and a voice from the back of the church called out, 'Yes, because she's already married to me and she's been having it off with you since Epiphany.' Sadly – at least from this book's standpoint – the accusation was a fabrication, a 'joke that misfired' according to the perpetrator who immediately apologized to all concerned and admitted he'd been at the champagne before the ceremony.

Some clergymen get away with the most outrageous behaviour, but very few. Back in 1535 a Catholic priest named Caldelamar was found guilty by an ecclesiastical tribunal in Toledo of frequenting brothels, assaulting women and extorting favours for others in exchange for absolution. For these offences he was condemned to thirty days house arrest and fined two ducats. Nowadays such clerical indulgence doesn't come so cheap. In Los Angeles in February 1984 a twenty-two-year-old former choir girl who claimed she was seduced by seven Catholic priests sued them and their Californian archdiocese for $21,000,000! Miss Rio Milla claimed that one of the priests was also the father of her sixteen-month-old baby, but she couldn't be sure which of the Magnificent Seven it was. The hanky-panky began in the confessional – of course – when Miss Milla maintains she was seduced by Father Santiago Tamayo who allegedly fondled her breasts through the confessional screen. Apparently Father Tamayo sub-sequently introduced her to half a dozen of his mates and then there was no stopping them. Miss Milla, who naturally enough had always wanted to be a nun, went along with it all at the time because she respected the priests' authority. 'I felt they would know what is a sin,' she said.

Clearly Miss Milla's case counts as a great sexual disaster whichever way you look at it, but with other cases assessing their validity for inclusion hasn't been easy. On the basis that if the Archbishop of Canterbury shot his mother-in-law at a hundred paces with an air gun, he could be described as a great shot but not necessarily as a great man, I have looked for stories where the average reaction might be 'Oh great!' rather than tragedies involving great issues or disasters that were of truly great moment to the individuals involved. That's why I am not going to pass on the details of the pathetic story of the priest who changed sex and when told he couldn't then become a nun committed suicide, while I cherish the cutting about the late Rector of Wrex-ham who was in bed with the wife (his own), no doubt being fruitful and multiplying, when he suddenly remem-bered he was supposed to be in church officiating at a christening. He threw off his wife – who had been a missionary, *on my word of honour* – threw on his clothes and rushed over from the rectory to the church only thirty yards away. It wasn't until he reached the font and confronted the congregation that he realized he had donned shoes, socks, shirt and surplice, but nothing else at all! According to the local newspaper, nobody took offence and the Rector was good-humoured and unrepentant. 'After all,' he said, 'I was almost certainly wearing more than John the Baptist ever did.'

Priests may think and talk about sex a great deal, but doctors are even more actively involved. Not only are they constantly handling naked bodies, for generations now they have also been regarded as unofficial marriage guidance counsellors. It is a role fraught with danger, as the great physician Sir James Paget explained to his students a century ago: 'Many of your patients will ask you about sexual intercourse, and expect you to prescribe fornication. I would just as soon prescribe theft or lying, or anything else that God has forbidden.'

Quite so.

You will recall the case of the nubile patient who arrived for a check-up and was invited to strip off by the young GP. She undressed and sat down. 'Big breaths,' said the doctor. 'Yes, aren't they?' said the girl. STOP! This is the sort of thing I have tried to avoid, I assure you. Occasionally an apocryphal anecdote may have slipped through the net, but despite tremendous temptation I have done my best to avoid too many old chestnuts. This is a collection of true stories and I have authenticated each one where possible. For example, I know the tale of the two medics caught copulating in the operating theatre at the Johns Hopkins Hospital in Baltimore is true because the visiting Professor of Obstetrics told me. The young couple slipped discreetly into the theatre to unwind after an exhausting twelve-hour night duty and were totally naked, contentedly canoodling on the operating table at seven in the morning when the darkened room was suddenly set ablaze with light as the professor and half their fellow students marched in to prepare for an early morning operation. At least it was a hysterectomy.

Young doctors have quite a reputation as sexual enthusiasts. So do politicians. A lust for lust seems to go hand in hand with a lust for power, and the catalogue of

Members of Parliament and Senators caught with their trousers down is a long one. Those who climb to the top of the greasy pole in politics seem better at concealing their sexual disasters than some of the smaller fry. Lloyd George was one of Britain's randiest premiers: he was once caught naked in bed with two girls whose combined age was less than half his. It was in his constituency and the disaster was that neither of the rare bits was Welsh. Lloyd George's amorous adventures went largely unreported during his lifetime, as did the remarkable sexual athleticism of the United States' most potent President, John F. Kennedy, described by one US senator as having 'the most active libido of any man I've ever known'. Kennedy's conquests ranged from Harlem prostitutes to Marilyn Monroe, but the nearest he got to a true sexual disaster was when he was almost caught with his pants around his ankles in a cupboard in a hotel in New Orleans. He was in there making love to Miss Blaze Starr while her fiancé, Governor Earl Long of Louisiana, was entertaining his guests in the adjoining room. Clearly Kennedy had a keen sense of history because, according to Miss Blaze, among the sweet nothings he whispered to her was the story of how Nan Brinton made love to President Harding in a closet in the White House. It's clearly a presidential tradition. They call it cupboard love.

By all accounts, Jack Kennedy loved dirty limericks. His brother Teddy is less fond of poetry, probably because of the success of this memorable verse by Leonard Miall:

> Tiddely Quiddely
> Edward M. Kennedy
> Quite unaccountably
> Drove in a stream.
>
> Pleas of amnesia
> Incomprehensible
> Possibly shattered
> Political dream.

While President Kennedy's sexual near-disaster qualifies for inclusion here, I don't think the sexual activities of his younger brother do. The same goes – but for different reasons – for the two most celebrated cases in recent British political history. John Profumo is one of the most charming men I've met – naturally, *that* was part of the problem – but there is nothing intrinsically comic about the Profumo Affair. Equally charming and even better looking is Cecil Parkinson. I was at a dinner with him the night before the news broke of his affair with his former secretary. Knowing nothing about it, I was terribly impressed at the way he hopped up between courses to phone either his wife or the Prime Minister. I felt his devotion to duty was admirable. Of course, the idea of a middle-aged man being pursued by a wife, a mistress *and* Margaret Thatcher does have comic potential, but the fact of there now being a real live baby in the case rather wipes the silly smirk off one's face.

Don't think I condone loose behaviour. Most certainly I don't. I almost go along with the judge who declared in court, 'I am not very sympathetic to couples living together when they are not married. I think it is immoral and can lead to crime.' Yes indeed, but it must be said that a man couldn't murder his wife unless he was married to her and the statistics clearly show that spouses murder each other much more frequently than live-in lovers do. Nevertheless, I'm a firm believer in marriage. I regard it as a fine institution, though my enthusiasm for it is as nothing compared with that of the retired US clergyman Glynn de Moss Wolfe who has been married twenty-five times to twenty-three different brides. He looks on his many marriages as equal triumphs (and keeps wedding dresses of differing sizes hanging in his wardrobe for ready use), whereas the world's most frequently married woman, Mrs Beverley Nina Avery, a barmaid from Los Angeles, regards most of her marriages as total disasters. Following her latest appearance in the divorce court, she claimed that all her fourteen husbands had broken her heart and five of them had also broken her nose.

Husbands and wives as experienced as Mr Wolfe and Mrs Avery need no advice from me, though I think we could all benefit from the wisdom of Dr Glass who counselled the readers of *The Times Educational Supplement* recently: 'Leave your sex organs with your bedroom slippers and your day's work will be far more productive and rewarding.' Yes, but will it be as much fun? More worldly, and doubtless more useful, is the advice Laurence Olivier was offered when a young man: 'Never, *never* have your wife in the morning in case something better turns up during the day.'

I am sorry to say continent husbands do not loom large in the pages that follow. From all I've heard they don't loom large in life either. I am afraid it appears that most modern marriages, even if they are not open, are certainly ajar. It's been the same for generations. The touching farewell scene between King George II and his dying Queen was only marred by her suggestion that he should remarry, and his firm refusal, 'Never, I will always take mistresses,' and her tart reply, 'That shouldn't hamper your marrying.'

Husbands and wives when caught by their wives and husbands *in delicto flagrante* with third parties occasionally contrive the most astonishing excuses. One young wife caught starkers with her boyfriend explained demurely to her husband that the naked man in the bedroom was her new osteopath and that he'd had to remove his trousers because he'd spilt coffee on them – which was *entirely* the husband's fault as he'd been promising to mend the leaky percolator for months. And a Californian film director told me on his honour (yes, I wondered about that too) that he managed to avert disaster when his wife came into his study unexpectedly and found him being indulged in fellatio by a young actress. 'Don't worry, darling,' he told his wife, 'it's nothing serious. I'm casting for the remake of *Deep Throat*.' Apparently, she swallowed it.

When caught in a compromising position Isadora Duncan declared, 'There's nothing to worry about. He's really a Greek god in disguise.' And there was the case recently of the young British army officer found trouserless and under the bed by an irate husband, who understandably assumed he had been cuckolded. Asked to explain himself, the officer

pulled on his pants and whispered to the husband confiden-
tially, 'I must ask you to keep this absolutely quiet, sir. It's
all part of an SAS training exercise. Very hush-hush.' The
incident took place in Dunstable, but it was during the
Falklands war, which must have helped.

Sexual disasters can occur in the most unlikely locations.
My assiduous reading of the back numbers of the racier
newspapers has taught me that people can have it away
almost anywhere: in 1967 in Nevada a young couple were
taken by surprise – and for a ride – when the crate they had
climbed into at nightfall was swept into the air at daybreak.
Inadvertently the young lovers had taken refuge in the
cradle of a gas balloon and during the stormy night the
moorings had come adrift. In 1972 in Brisbane another
couple were arrested for fornicating in a phone box. They
were discharged with a caution when they explained to the
police court that they were homeless and had carefully
checked that the telephone was out of order first. In 1981 in
London another Australian couple were having a high old
time in the back of their Range Rover parked in Mayfair. An
hour later they were still hard at it – but in Mile End. The
police had towed the vehicle away not realizing that the
owners were in the back.

There have been reports of people caught in the act in
almost every conceivable location – yes, even at a Family
Planning Clinic in Mortimer Street, London. Incredibly,
among the more popular setting for sexual encounters –
especially among younger lovers – are graveyards and mor-
tuaries. I suppose they reckon they won't be disturbed. Less
macabre and even more popular as a locale for love-making
is the bathroom, though not everyone approves of sex in the
bath. Following the major oil price hike in December 1973
there were worldwide campaigns designed to encourage
people to save energy. In Britain the South Eastern Gas
Board thought it would do its best for the cause by running
an advertisement featuring a couple sitting in the same bath.
Ran the slogan: 'Put a little romance into your bath by
sharing the water.' Members of Parliament were not

amused. Conservative MP John Stokes thundered: 'It is deplorably vulgar and in the worst possible taste.' A fellow MP, Joseph Kinsey, was equally outraged: 'I am shocked,' he said. 'It is debasing the standards of the Gas Board to suggest that we should share our baths.' Public opinion, however, begged to differ, and the proverbial man in the street was quoted as saying: 'People have been sharing a bath for years. There is nothing wrong in it. It is better than having a rubber duck.'

That said, if you bath with a duck you're less likely to end up in the divorce court. Mrs Cheryl Wentworth was sued for divorce by her husband after he had returned home to find her in the tub with her lover, a thirty-six-year-old brush salesman, who gloried in the name of Mike Rover. The errant lovers wouldn't have been in such hot water had not Mr Rover slipped a disc while making love to Mrs Wentworth in the bath and the pair of them consequently been imprisoned there. Poor Mr Wentworth suffered not only the humiliation of finding his wife in the bath with another man, he also suffered the indignity of having to prise them apart and help the randy Rover out of the water.

Another painful incident was reported in Broadstairs in Kent. A thirty-three-year-old housewife (whose name didn't appear in the cutting – which is a shame because she sounds fun) was upstairs in the bath and totally forgot that the window cleaner was due. Sure enough, this was the day when every window cleaner's fantasy came true and the young man climbed his ladder to find himself gazing into the bathroom where the attractive housewife was happily engaged in sudsing her charms. Showing little or no surprise at finding the window cleaner gawping in at her, Mrs X apparently decided to entertain him to a soapy cabaret. Enchanted by the bubble-bath peepshow the window cleaner understandably felt he should reciprocate in some way and proceeded to undo his trousers. Unfortunately, the unzipping combined with the excitement were too much for him, or at least for his ladder – which fell away from the wall and crashed into the neighbour's greenhouse. It was this accident that brought the window cleaner to court in a wheelchair. The magistrate wished him a speedy recovery and fined him £15.

It's not only anonymous window cleaners in Broadstairs whose dignity has been dented by bathtub disasters. Sir John Gielgud was one of a number of distinguished actors who were persuaded to appear in the notorious *Penthouse*-produced movie *Caligula*. 'I played a whole scene in a bath of tepid water,' Gielgud recalls. 'It took three days to shoot and every two hours some terrible hags dragged me out, rubbed me down and put me back into the water again. Most extraordinary proceedings.' In fact, the behaviour on the set was relatively decorous when Gielgud was around. When shooting a different scene on another day the director Tinto Brass had oral sex with a *Penthouse* Pet in front of the entire crew to show the cast the effect he was after. Mrs Brass took her husband's behaviour in her stride: 'He was just being his usual extrovert self.' For another *Penthouse* Pet real disaster struck when she was required to pee on one of the actors in one of the movie's more torrid scenes. The director wanted to shoot the sequences in three takes. The first and second went swimmingly. For the third take, the girl wasn't supposed to pee, but she did. Tinto Brass screeched at her, 'For Chrissakes, you want to be an actress but you can't even take a "don't piss" direction!'

It was another great entertainer, Maurice Chevalier, who observed, 'Many a man has fallen in love with a girl in a light so dim he would not have chosen a suit by it.' It's certainly true that when the lights are out anything can happen. One husband I know came home late and unexpectedly, undressed, clambered into bed and found himself snuggling up to his wife's lover. What makes the story truly alarming is that he didn't realize his mistake till daybreak.

In the course of my researches I have come across several tales of people climbing into other people's beds and being none the wiser until one or other of the parties sensed it was all going much more entertainingly than usual. Whether we like it or not, whether we can see it or not, there's no denying that variety is the spice of sex. Darkness can cover a multitude of sins so when the wrong body is found in the bed it isn't always an accident. In the 1880s a middle-aged actor who had recently appeared in *Measure for Measure* took his cue from the plot and successfully bedded an ambitious young actress as a result. She was an ardent admirer of Sir Henry Irving and the middle-aged actor assured her that he could improve her prospects by bringing her to the great actor's bed. When she arrived the boudoir was in darkness and the unknown actor played Sir Henry's part to the full.

It was a near contemporary of Henry Irving's, Mrs Patrick Campbell, who declared, 'It doesn't matter what you do in the bedroom so long as you don't do it in the street and frighten the horses.' I agree. And so did Detective Joseph Leary of the New York police who arrested two men and a woman for disturbing the peace in a street in Manhattan. The woman, a twenty-seven-year-old model, Jan Tice, was standing naked on a street corner, while one of the men photographed her and the other gave directions. They claimed they were preparing a book about the city's famous buildings with photographs of the shapely Jan as a decoration to each subject. Detective Leary was unimpressed, but when they came to court the judge was more sympathetic. He threw out the case, arguing that no offence had been committed because the public was not watching. 'The defendants annoyed no one, interfered with no one, obstructed no one, except perhaps the police officer,' he said. 'A breach of the peace requires the presence of the public. The public relates to people. There weren't any people there.'

When Fiona Richmond went bareback-riding in London's Piccadilly Circus the court wasn't so sympathetic. The trouble was that it was Miss Richmond whose back was bare and she drew quite a crowd. It seems the police can cope with naked horses – in fact they're seen on them regularly – but a naked rider is another matter. Naturally, Miss Richmond wasn't starkers on horseback just for the fun of it; she was out to promote one of the erotic entertainments mounted by Britain's soft-porn king, Paul

Raymond, one of the nicest men ever to give me a lift in his Rolls and champagne for Christmas.

Paul's a perfect gentleman and Fiona's a lovely lady. When I met her recently I told her it was the first time I'd seen her with her clothes on; then she introduced me to her husband. Despite her extensive experience of life, recounted so vividly over the years in the pages of *Men Only*, Fiona didn't have much to give me for *Great Sexual Disasters*. She's seen it all, of course ('And as for his sword: terifioso! Pale-coloured pure Toledo steel. Maybe not the largest but certainly the straightest I had ever seen'), but you won't find many details of her adventures here because, on the whole, she's been lucky in love.

The same goes for Ruby, a forty-four-year-old stripper and mother of three I met not long ago when we both were appearing at a nightclub in the North of England. We shared a dressing room – 'an undressing room, I call it', said Ruby with a cheerful chuckle, as she rubbed body make-up over her stretch-marks. 'Don't you regard it as something of a disaster having to strip at your age?' I asked with all the delicacy of a *News of the World* cub reporter. 'No, no, they love the fuller figure!' So saying she leant forward and pushed her ample bottom towards me. 'Would you sequin my bum, luv?' I did as she asked, but it wasn't as exciting as it sounds: what I had to do was apply glue to her buttocks and then stick on a sprinkling of sequins. 'They love to see your cheeks sparkle. It drives 'em wild!'

Truth to tell, Ruby's performance was greeted with respectful silence. About a month later I found myself addressing a rather livelier audience in a more salubrious setting: Leicester University. The occasion was a men-only dinner and two speakers had been booked: myself and Dr Rachel Jenkins, Reader in Mathematics at Swansea. I spoke my piece and it went well enough, though I was apprehensive as to the ride Dr Jenkins might get as the audience was fairly merry and seemed to be in the mood for ribaldry rather than a dissertation on the joys of higher mathematics. I needn't have worried. When her turn came, Dr Jenkins rose to her feet and began to deliver her address with singular authority. For the first two or three minutes all went well, then a loutish voice from the back called out, 'Get 'em off, darlin'!' Suddenly there was no holding them. From around the hall the cries came, 'Show us what you've got, Doctor! Give us a thrill, love! Go on, get em off! Off! OFF!' This was too much for Dr Jenkins. She clambered onto her chair and then onto the table in front of her and then – believe it or not, but I was there and *it is true* – took off every stitch of clothing before leaving the hall to the most tumultuous standing ovation I have ever been privileged to hear.

Over the years I have met a number of strippers and have always found them likeable people. I was fortunate in being able to take a semi-professional interest in their work in 1972 when that good and kind man, the Earl of Longford, KG, PC, invited me to become a member of his informal team investigating pornography. We were a motley group of intrepid investigators – our number included an Archbishop, a couple of ordinary bishops, a rabbi, Malcolm Muggeridge and Cliff Richard – but it was a happy experience for me and I still treasure the raincoat I bought at the time. Most of our work was done in London, in rooms kindly supplied by London University, where we would sit leafing through pornographic magazines and shaking our heads in disgust: 'Tut tut ... oh, dear ... how shaming ... my, my ... oh, look, Rabbi, one of yours!'

We did some field work in and around Soho as well, where we kept bumping into dirty old men in sex shops asking for free samples on the pretext that they were members of Lord Longford's team, but the highlight of the investigation was our expenses-paid trip to Denmark. We went to Copenhagen to reap the alien porn and what fun it was! For Lord Longford, of course, it was a sexual disaster and quite right too: it would have been an international scandal had it been anything else. He is an enchantingly innocent man – the only person I know who can embrace a totally naked woman and not notice it – and he went to the live sex-show in Copenhagen with what he called a 'fresh and open mind'. He soon walked out. The club's manager was deeply distressed. He assumed the gartered earl was a connoisseur who was stomping out dissatisfied and rushed up to him exclaiming, 'But you haven't seen the intercourse.' Lord Longford explained that he'd seen enough for science and more than enough for pleasure. I think he might also have seen the *News of the World* photographer lurking there. The star of the show – whip in hand – was mingling with the crowd and plonking herself down on the welcoming laps of members of the audience. Had she landed on Lord Longford's lap ... well, click, flash and around the world in eighty seconds would have gone pictures of elderly English milord with naked Danish dolly on his noble knee.

Not being an earl, and not wishing to show discourtesy to our hosts, I decided to stay for 'the intercourse', performed by a young couple from Roskilde who – to the amazement and indeed the envy of the British contingent – managed to keep it up for half an hour. Later I was introduced to the young people: she was a law student and just in it for the money, but he took the work more seriously. 'I'm a freelance and, of course, I have no job security. We do three shows a night and sometimes I find it difficult. We are a small club and there are no understudies. The boss says, "The show must go on." If I can't make it, I get the sack and that would be a disaster.'

If it's challenging work for the artistes, it isn't all plain sailing for the customers, either. Audience participation is expected and both men and women are invited up on stage to try their hand. At the performance I attended a middle-aged tourist from Omaha was brought, albeit reluctantly, into the spotlight. The leading lady lowered him gently onto a cushion and proceeded to undo his trousers. With a seraphic smile she turned to the rest of the audience and exclaimed delightedly, 'Oh, look everybody, isn't it sweet? It's the tiniest one I have seen all week!'

It was that great pioneer of striptease, Gypsy Rose Lee, who remarked, 'Men aren't attracted to me by my mind. They're attracted by what I don't mind.' That's the joy of most strippers: they may not be free but they're easy. It's the same with prostitutes. I went to see one in the course of my researches – what are expenses for, after all? – and she couldn't have been more welcoming: 'You've got to be relaxed about this job – easy come, easy go, that's my motto.' Welcoming she was, helpful she wasn't. When I asked her to recount her tales of sexual disaster for the book I was writing she simply assumed it was a ploy and that I was one of those 'kinky fellers who like to hear a girl talk dirty'. She obliged with a stream of fruity anecdotes, which I promise to pass on to you sometime, but which have no place here because not one of them can have had any basis in truth.

Most of the distinguished folk who have kindly given me stories to include in the book have asked to remain anonymous. Several of the friends who have contributed anecdotes – for example, Christopher Biggins, Simon Cadell and Noel Davis – I *can* acknowledge because they don't feature personally in any of the stories and their sex lives are generally known to be triumphant anyway. Happily, I can also acknowledge the unique contribution of Miss Nina Martyn. This beautiful girl and I were travelling on a train to Liverpool when the idea of a book of great sexual disasters came to us. There was nothing between us, you understand, but it was a long journey and Nina had come equipped for it with a pile of newspapers and magazines, so to entertain me she read out edited highlights from the problem pages. What inspired the book was the sad story of the unfortunate *Daily Star* reader who had written to the paper about his 'hair trigger problem'. Apparently, he was a hot-blooded husband and easily aroused. Indeed, he would get so excited so quickly that by the time he had undone his pyjama cord he was past the point of no return. As a consequence his wife was repeatedly left unsatisfied. How should he cope with this disaster? he asked. Get elasticated pyjamas was the *Star*'s stunning suggestion.

Judging from the correspondence columns of the

magazines and papers that specialize in such matters, men may be fascinated by the female anatomy but what really *obsesses* them is their own. As sex-change pioneer April Ashley put it to me, 'If a man doesn't have a really full basket he isn't much of a man' – and that from someone who has had it all off. (How *could* she? The idea of a vasectomy makes *me* wince.) While it is a truth universally acknowledged that with sex it is quality not quantity that counts, men still believe bigger is better and tend to regard anything less than the standard six inches (fifteen centimetres in Europe, but you know what these Continentals are) as cause for dismay. The man who could only boast half an inch at full stretch regarded it as a major disaster, but, interestingly enough, at the other extreme – and both these are the medically attested record-holders – the only man ever known (*reliably*) to have come up with thirteen inches also regarded it as a bit of a body blow.

A friend of mine from Oswego, New York, confided to me that when he went to a prostitute in Manhattan she had flattered him with gasps of amazement and then took her tape measure to him: 'Eight and a half inches – wow!' Being a vain man – actually, simply being a man – he boasted of this to his fiancée and on their honeymoon she too had produced a tape measure but came up with a mere five and a half inches. Nothing disreputable in that (eighty-seven per cent of adult American males fall within the five to seven inch range), but a long way off eight and a half. The explanation, of course, is that the prostitute had been using a special tape measure: it's called a Boostertape. They're made in New Jersey and are available from most leading sex stores.

The other disaster that men seem more prone to than women is 'loss of sexual prowess'. There are now clinics all over the world that specialize in reviving your lost libido. In search of a little rejuvenation Noel Coward went to one of the very best in Switzerland, where the basis of the treatment is to inject the patients with tiny doses of sheep's glands. As he drove through the gates of the clinic's beautiful estate, Coward noticed a flock of sheep grazing peacefully on the hillside. Right in the middle of the flock was a lone black ram. 'Ah,' said Coward, 'I see Paul Robeson is here already.'

Not everyone approves of the open discussion of such matters and if you're finding that the raunchy nature of some of the stories here isn't to your liking, do please pass the book on to one of your filthier-minded friends. On the other hand, knowing that the Hertfordshire Trading Standards Office in St Albans recently received a complaint from a pensioner who had bought two pornographic videos and had been gravely disappointed because they were not explicit enough, I am also aware that I may be disappointing some readers by not providing sufficient lurid detail. All I can say is that, bearing in mind Groucho Marx's observation, 'Whoever named it necking was a poor judge of anatomy', I have at least done my best to avoid too many euphemisms while trying to produce a slim volume that aims to be frank and fun rather than frank and fearless.

I have written books on a wide variety of topics, from prisons to pantomime, but this is the one on which the research work has been the most rewarding. *Great Sexual Disasters* has taken me down some truly delightful byways. For example, looking into the background of the couple whose marriage broke down because they gave each other a severe electric shock every time they kissed, I unearthed a cornucopia of fascinating facts about the pleasures and pitfalls of kissing ... in 1656 Captain Kemble of Boston was sentenced to two hours in the stocks for 'lewd and unseemly behaviour' because he kissed his wife in public on the Sabbath after a three-year absence at sea ... rather more recently, in 1965, a man caught kissing in public in Kuwait was jailed for three and a half years ... in 1969 the police chief in the town of Inca on the island of Majorca launched a crack-down on couples kissing in public: offenders were fined 500 pesetas per kiss and the thirty rebellious couples who started a protest kiss-in at the harbour at Cala Figuera were arrested and fined a total of 45,000 pesetas ... in 1980 in Tokyo Yukiko Nagata and Toshiaki Shirai narrowly escaped drowning when they held a kiss underwater for two minutes eighteen seconds ... in 1980 in Singer Island, Florida, Debbie Luray and Jim Schuyler suffered from exhaustion after kissing non-stop for five days and twelve hours ... according to Dr Malcolm Katz of Toronto, Canada, even moderate kissing is dangerous and can reduce the average lover's lifespan by at least ten minutes each year...

Oh yes, *Great Sexual Disasters* has taught me a lot – including the Swiss Kiss (it's a French kiss through which you yodel) – but the most useful lesson I think I've learnt is this: when faced with a potential sexual disaster, keep your cool. Remember the great example of Chico Marx who when caught kissing a chorus girl turned to his wife and explained: 'I wasn't kissing her. I was whispering in her mouth.'

PART 2
Dishing the Dirt

OH, CALAMITY!

'Did you hear about the fellow who blamed arithmetic for his divorce? His wife put two and two together.'

Earl Wilson

'Put it this way, Bristow – she finds the pen is mightier than the sword.'

The lesson this book has to teach is that none of us is immune from disaster. Young or old, straight or gay, philanderer or flasher – we're all vulnerable. Even the most devoted married couple isn't safe...

In June 1977 Monsieur and Madame Philippe Dubois spent their honeymoon on the French Indian Ocean island of Réunion. One night Monsieur Dubois went for a walk. On his return he decided to surprise his bride by leaping over the fence surrounding their rented cottage.

No doubt one fence looks much like another in moonlit Réunion, which was unfortunate for poor Philippe whose amorous enthusiasm led him to jump into the crater of a volcano from which he never emerged.

You don't have to be a budding Casanova to court disaster, but it helps... In March 1980 a Perth businessman who had been eyeing his secretary for almost longer than his desire could stand was thrilled when she invited him back to her home on the evening of his birthday.

It was clear from her conversation in the taxi that the young lady was doing her utmost to make him feel relaxed and by the time they reached her flat he was convinced that she was giving him the come-on. Her behaviour inside the apartment was equally encouraging. She gave him a large whisky, invited him to take off his jacket and tie, and then left him for a moment while she 'went into the bedroom to see to a couple of things'. This was all the encouragement he needed. Determined to take full advantage of this unexpected treat, he didn't stop at his jacket and tie.

All he was wearing was his wristwatch when the bedroom door opened and in walked his four-year-old son, carrying a birthday cake, followed by his wife, secretary and colleagues from the office, singing 'Happy Birthday to You...'

It is something of a relief to discover that the love-life of the original Casanova (baptized, Giovanni, 1725; died, exhausted, 1798) wasn't all a bed of roses. Although only 116 of the thousands of women who fell under his spell have been named in published records, there is at least one that even he would have preferred to have remained veiled in obscurity. She was the entrancing young mistress of the Duke of Matalone, a seventeen-year-old beauty named Leonilda, whom Casanova first met on a visit to the Duke in Venice.

So struck with her was the great amorist and adventurer that he took the unprecedented step of asking the Duke to release Leonilda so that Casanova could marry her himself. The Duke graciously gave his consent. Provided Leonilda's mother raised no objections Casanova was as good as married. The Duke would arrange for Casanova to meet his future mother-in-law that same evening. When they came face to face in the drawing room just before going in to dinner, Anna Maria Vallati took one look at the man her daughter was to marry, screamed and fainted. Casanova, it appeared, had been equally smitten by *her* charms eighteen years earlier and the lovely Leonilda was living proof of the ardour of his passion. Hoist by his own petard, so to speak, the over-amorous father had been about to wed and bed his own delightful daughter.

From Verona's Romeo to Rome's Marcello Mastroianni, Italians have long had a reputation as outstanding lovers. The language helps. Call Giovanni Casanova 'John New-house' and immediately he loses some of his romantic allure. Of course, it isn't necessarily an advantage to belong to a nation noted for sexual athleticism. According to Mastroianni, 'Once they call you a Latin lover you're in real trouble. Women expect an Oscar performance in bed – every time!'

By contrast, other less honest, and far less distinguished, Italians have taken unscrupulous advantage of their country's passionate reputation. A few years ago advertisements from love-sick Italian girls in search of 'Mr Right' started appearing in a number of European magazines. The ads offered the Common Market's lonely bachelors the sweethearts of their dreams. Would-be husbands were invited to write to the girls of their choice and hundreds did so. Each suitor received an encouraging reply in which his young lady offered to travel to meet him – the only snag being that she hadn't the money to pay for the fare. Could her suitor send it? He could indeed! Scores of men from all over the Continent posted what amounted to several thousand pounds to their Italian fiancées elect.

What none of the men knew was that they were all mailing the money to the same address in Salerno. Having sent their cheques they heard no more. It took Calogero Contrino, an Italian working in Germany, to discover exactly what was going on.

Signor Contrino had posted the best part of £200 to his girl friend, and had followed this with repeated love letters, none of which had received a reply. In the end he travelled down to Salerno to see for himself what had happened to his loved one. He went to her address and was appalled to find that she appeared to live inside the city's prison. He soon discovered that all the other 'girls' lived with her.

The magazine advertisements had been placed not by nubile lonely lovelies, but by five prison inmates on remand.

The French too have an enviable reputation as lovers ... Witness the case of young Jacques Piret, a fledgeling *gendarme* from Toulouse. Piret was alone on the beat for the first time when he noticed an illegally parked car outside a smart boutique in the centre of town. He had been warned to keep an eye open for this vehicle and for its attractive driver, the boutique owner herself, Madame Evelyne Laforge. She habitually left her car in this no-parking zone and in the past had nonchalantly thrown away the dozens of parking tickets that had been taped to her windscreen. Suddenly seeing Madame Laforge approaching her car, the ambitious young policeman sensed that this was his chance to impress his superiors. Seizing the moment, he moved in to tackle the lady.

When it came to dealing with policemen – especially policemen as inexperienced and impressionable as Jacques Piret – Madame Laforge was no novice. Piret had barely started giving her a mild reprimand when she burst into tears and showed every sign of becoming hysterical. The lady's ranting and screaming and the young policeman's increasingly desperate efforts to soothe her attracted quite a crowd. When Piret threatened to take Madame Laforge down to the station he found the onlookers starting to turn against him. The situation was only saved by Piret offering to drive the distraught Madame Laforge home in her car.

As they drove along, the lady recovered some of her composure and when they stopped she apologized to the badly shaken policeman and invited him inside to discuss the matter of the unpaid fines over a drink. Seduced by Madame Laforge's bewitching smile, Piret forgot both himself and the regulations about not drinking on duty, and followed the lady into her house.

Madame Laforge entertained him beautifully and he quickly warmed to her cause. So warm did he get that when Monsieur Philippe Laforge got home from work he found his wife half-dressed in the bedroom and less than thrilled to see him. Young Piret was discovered in the wardrobe dressed only in his underpants and holding his carefully folded uniform over his arm. At this point he abandoned standard police procedures altogether and made a bolt for the door hotly pursued by the furious husband. Out in the street Piret produced his gun and fired a warning shot into the air as he ran down the pavement naked but for his Y-fronts.

He got away from Monsieur Laforge, but not, alas, from the long arm of the law. A court fined him the equivalent of £50 for 'outraging public decency' and he was drummed out of the force after being found guilty of a 'wrongful use of his firearm'. His promising career had been nipped in the bud because, in the words of the presiding judge, 'Gendarme Piret was carried away by an excess of zeal.'

While in France the police (or at least one of them) are turning from crime to sex, in Germany the criminals (or at least some of them) are doing exactly the same. In Frankfurt recently, three burglars, two men and a girl, broke into a leading store one night and made their way to the cashier's office. As they were passing through the furniture department one of the men and a girl paused for a little slap and tickle on a sofa. The third member of the gang asked if he could join in and was told there wasn't room. Angry and hurt he ditched the earlier plan, found a phone and telephoned the police to tell them there was a robbery taking place. Then he made his getaway. A few minutes later his partners in crime were arrested, naked and preoccupied.

Austria's contemporary answer to Casanova is Heinrich Schwab of Vienna, who came to grief one afternoon when he and his current mistress were disturbed by the unexpected return of her husband. Naked and trapped in the bedroom Schwab had no alternative but to grab his clothes and wriggle under the bed until the coast was clear. It turned out that the husband, a travelling salesman, had come home with the sole intention of going to bed himself, not with his wife but with a heavy cold.

Knowing of the husband's intense jealousy and violent temper, Herr Schwab opted to wait until morning before making his escape. However, come daybreak the husband still felt pretty groggy and decided to stay tucked up for the day. Schwab, naked and afraid, remained beneath the bed all the while. By nightfall, the husband was feeling much better, but as it was now dark there wasn't much point in his rising so he stayed in bed until his wife joined him. Schwab, paralysed with cold, stiffness and his desperate efforts to stifle the calls of nature, was forced to stay put for another twelve hours, until mercifully the husband rose from his sick-bed, dressed and left for work.

The moment he heard the front door slam the frantic Schwab crawled out from under the bed. He had just begun restoring circulation to parts of his body that had long since given up hope of seeing blood again when the bedroom door opened and the husband nipped back for his car keys.

Whatever their nationality, very few people are consistently lucky in love, but some do seem to be unluckier than most. A few years ago the *Whitley Bay Guardian* carried the remarkable story of a railway worker's attempts to commit suicide after failing to win the heart of a girl he had met at his station. Interviewed by a reporter the railwayman catalogued his dismal failures, beginning: 'At 7.30 I had a drink and walked into the sea but it was so wet I turned back, went home and by 9.15 I had wired up my easy chair to the mains. However, each time I threw the switch the power fused. Following this, I broke my Gaye-way mirror and tried to cut my wrists, yet somehow the slashes were not deep enough. After that I tried to hang myself from the banisters; unfortunately the knot was improperly tied. Finally I surrounded myself with cushions and set them on fire. This method was much too hot, so I jumped out of the window and telephoned the Samaritans but they were constantly engaged.'

Getting your girl isn't always easy. Keeping her once you've got her can be even more difficult. The boyfriends of Pauline Bonaparte – the younger sister of the Emperor Napoleon – had a wonderful time banging into her, but a terrible time hanging onto her. Known from Haiti to St Helena as an insatiable sexpot, she had a couple of husbands, countless lovers and a high old time until she died at the early age of forty-four, after nearly thirty years of non-stop fornication. Prince Camillo Borghese, her hapless second husband, was banished from her bed because his penis was '*si drollement petit*', but however well-endowed you were your chances of maintaining a lasting relationship with Pauline were slim. She was fair, but she was fickle. She fell passionately in love with a Commissioner of the Convention named Fréron and wrote to him in one of her letters: 'I love you always and most passionately. I love you forever, my beautiful idol, my heart, my appealing lover. I love you, love you, the most loved of lovers, and I swear never to love anyone else!'

She kept her word – for a fortnight. Within two weeks of declaring her undying devotion to Commissioner Fréron she gave her heart and soul (yes, and everything else) to Anoche Junot, the military hero who became her brother's adjutant in Egypt and later a field marshal.

Napoleon himself was more constant than his sister. He took the same number of wives, but far fewer mistresses – probably no more than forty during the fifty-one years of his life. His first wife, of course, was the notorious Josephine de Beauharnais. She was thirty-two and a seasoned woman of the world when they married. Their wedding night was lively, but not totally satisfactory. Disaster struck in the form of Josephine's pet dog, Fortuné, who assumed his mistress was being attacked by the naked Napoleon and successfully dampened the bridegroom's ardour by jumping onto the nuptial bed and biting him just as he was about to take advantage of his newly acquired conjugal rights.

Napoleon and Josephine had no children, but despite her jibes – '*Bonaparte est bon-à-rien*' was her favourite line – he wasn't impotent. He had a couple of offspring by Marie Walewska, his best-loved mistress, and a legitimate heir by his second wife, Marie Louise of Austria. When Napoleon married her she was a total innocent: not only had she not seen a naked man before, she had never been permitted to look upon a naked male animal either!

For the Emperor Napoleon the final sexual humiliation came one hundred and fifty years after his death. In 1972 his inch-long penis was offered for auction at Christies in London, but failed to reach the reserve price.

It doesn't take much to bring a man down to size. In 1980, Julie Barlow, an anthropology student at the University of Chicago, was stepping out of a phone booth one evening when a man approached her displaying himself and asking, 'What do you think of that then?'

'It looks like a cock to me,' she said, 'only smaller.'

The phenomenon of people exposing themselves in public places is not to be encouraged, but there's no denying it does happen and it isn't easy knowing what is best to do when unexpectedly faced with a 'flasher'. Not long ago, a letter in the London *Daily Mail* discussed some of the niceties involved when dealing with the situation on a golf course:

'I read with interest of the lady golfer who, when confronted by a naked man wearing only a bowler hat, asked him whether he was a member, and then hit him with a Number 8 iron.

'Purists will long dispute whether it was obviously a mashie-shot, or whether the niblick should have been used. I hold no strong views myself, but I do wonder what the lady would have done had the man produced from his bowler hat a valid membership card.'

'Flashing' is no laughing matter. It can cause considerable distress. Some years ago, three redoubtable ladies of the English theatre – Joyce Carey, Peggy Ashcroft and Edith Evans – were appearing in a play together in the West End. Joyce Carey, like many of her theatrical contemporaries, was living in Brighton at the time and commuted to town for performances. One Saturday she arrived for the matinée in a state of acute distress. Indeed, she was so shaken and incoherent that the stage manager feared he might have to cancel the performance, which was drawing perilously close. In the distance he could hear the murmur of middle-aged ladies ordering their trays of tea for the interval and settling into the red plush with their boxes of chocolates. Feeling at a total loss since Joyce refused to explain her problem to him the stage manager called for Peggy Ashcroft who rushed straight round to Miss Carey's dressing room.

'Joyce, dear, what's happened, you look awful?'

'Oh, Peggy,' sobbed Joyce, 'the most terrible thing ... I was all alone in the carriage ... with this man ... Just as we entered a tunnel he stood up and ... and EXPOSED himself. It was quite, quite dreadful.'

After trying to calm her down Peggy Ashcroft went off to find her a glass of brandy and coming back met Edith Evans on the stairs. Seeing the brandy, the formidable Dame Edith demanded imperiously, '*What* is going on? *Who* is drinking brandy before a matinée?'

'It's for Joyce, Edith, she's had a terrible experience.'

Followed by Peggy Ashcroft, Dame Edith proceeded at once to Joyce Carey's dressing room and demanded, 'What's all this about your having a terrible experience, Joyce?' Joyce Carey went through her story again in a calmer but still tremulous voice.

There was a mere second's pause before Dame Edith enquired solicitously, 'Well, and where exactly *was* this tunnel?'

Disaster can strike anywhere at any time. In Australia recently an early morning jogger was taking his usual run through a suburb of Melbourne when he passed a lone car parked by the side of the road, its windows well steamed up. Forty minutes later the jogger passed the same car on his way back home and this time he noticed faint signs of life inside, accompanied by pathetic cries. He stopped, peered into the car and found a half-naked couple locked together on the back seat.

'Christ! Thank God someone's come,' said the man. 'My back went hours ago and I haven't been able to move.'

'Nor have I!' said an exasperated female voice from somewhere underneath.

The jogger ran off to call the police, who took one look at the car and called the fire service and an ambulance. The fire chief consulted the ambulance man, decided the patient couldn't be moved without severe risk and ordered the top of the car to be cut open to free him.

By the time this had been done and the ambulance crew had lifted the man free a sizeable crowd had gathered, much to the lovers' embarrassment. 'I'm sorry about this, lady,' said one of the policemen, 'but at least he hasn't come to any more harm this way.'

'To hell with him,' she said. 'How am I going to explain to my husband what's happened to the car?'

In Britain smart country houses have more than once proved to be the setting for great sexual disasters. Back in the 'naughty nineties' Lord Charles Beresford met a charming fellow guest at The Vyne in Hampshire, the home of his friend Sir Charles Chute. The flirtatious lady generously offered to further their acquaintance after everyone had gone to bed and whispered explicit instructions on how to reach her bedroom.

When the coast was clear Lord Charles slipped out of his own bedroom and, following her directions to the letter, furtively made his way towards his lady's chamber. Once outside her door he eagerly pulled off his dressing gown and pyjamas, lifted the latch, nipped into the room and made a passionate lunge for the bed. Somewhere along the line he must have lost his way – at least that was the gist of what the Bishop of Chester said when he found himself suddenly pounced on by a naked man in the middle of the night.

A few years later, during an idyllic week-end party at Chatsworth, one of the youngest and prettiest guests made a secret assignation with a dashing naval officer, and to help him find his way to her room promised to leave an unremarkable yet unmistakable marker outside her room: a plate of smoked salmon sandwiches.

The party broke up and the guests retired in the small hours of the morning. The lady lay in a fever of anticipation as the great house settled down to sleep. By two all was silent. By three the lovely girl was almost beside herself. She held out for another forty minutes before daring to open her bedroom door and peer down the moonlit corridor. There was no sign of her lover, nor, at her feet, of the smoked salmon sandwiches.

She left Chatsworth at first light, broken-hearted. Her wretched amour followed a few hours later, equally downcast. Neither of them was to know that the cause of their frustration was a fellow guest who, on his way to bed, had felt a little peckish.

Non-consummation can be a disaster. So too can be the over-enthusiastic anticipation of consummation.

Tim Brooke-Taylor tells the story of a Cambridge friend – 'a friend, you understand' – who had been fixed up with a blind date. An eternal optimist, the young man popped into the chemist's during the afternoon before meeting the girl and bought a packet of contraceptives.

That evening when he went to meet his blind date he recognized her immediately. She worked at the chemist's and had served him earlier in the day.

Disaster can strike when you least expect it – and least deserve it ... David Green, Vice-President of Sales for a food-canning corporation based in New Orleans, had been away on a business trip to St Louis and had promised his wife, Lindsay, that he would be home on an early evening flight. He missed it but couldn't reach her before she left for the airport to meet him.

When Lindsay found that her husband wasn't on the

flight as planned she sent cables to five of his friends and business associates in St Louis saying: 'David not home. Is spending night with you?' Then she got in her car and drove back to the house.

David arrived home by cab a couple of hours later, having caught the next flight. He found his wife standing at the door holding five telegrams that had just been delivered. Each one simply said 'Yes'.

Disaster can strike at any age ... When a seventy-six-year-old Greek woman was refused permission to marry her eighty-four-year-old fiancé by her eighty-six-year-old brother, she persuaded her man to elope with her. The wily brother suspected that she might try something like this and waited to catch the luckless maid.

He pounced as they were coming down a ladder from her bedroom at night. The lover slipped on the bottom rung, fell over and broke his ankle and the brother, unbalanced by the sudden burst of activity, tripped over him and broke a leg.

The two men ended up side by side in hospital where the sister came and held hands with both of them.

Disaster can strike even when you're innocent ... A young English housewife of unblemished reputation had just climbed into her bath one afternoon when she remembered the cake she had left in the oven. Naked, she nipped downstairs to rescue the cake before it burned and was just putting it in the larder when there was a noise at the back door – the butcher coming to deliver her weekly order! She knew he would leave it on the kitchen table if there was no answer, so she hid in the broom cupboard. To her dismay the footsteps didn't stop at the table but carried on towards her hiding place. There they halted and the cupboard door opened to reveal the electricity man who had come to read the meter.

'I was expecting the butcher,' she explained.

FOR BETTER,
FOR WORSE

'She said he proposed something on
their wedding night her own brother
wouldn't have suggested.'

James Thurber

'I love you too, Leonie, but I keep falling out of bed.'

'I fell in love with my husband simply because he was so different from every other boy I had ever met. He did not like love-making, neither did I. Now after twenty-six years of marriage I sometimes wonder if I have missed something, but I am happy. He's a wonderful husband. He never actually proposed, but we saw a three-piece suite we both liked and that clinched the deal.'

There's happiness for you! Not many wives could send such a contented letter to their favourite women's weekly. For most people making the ideal match isn't so easy: sadly, there aren't enough three-piece suites to go round.

In an imperfect world, how *does* one set about finding the perfect partner?

In 1981 Vincent Lowe Jr of Scottsdale, Arizona, approached a total stranger in the street and asked her to marry him. She said yes. As he explained to the court hearing his divorce some six weeks later, 'It was my thirtieth birthday and I was feeling depressed because I wasn't married. I went out for a walk and saw this great-looking girl coming out of a hotel. I thought, "That's the wife for me," and went over and proposed. Doreen accepted me immediately, and we were married by special licence three days later. As you can imagine, when I discovered on our wedding night that Doreen, though legally a woman, was in all other respects a man in drag, I was deeply disappointed.'

One way of meeting potential partners is to advertise for them. The first woman to place a lonely-hearts advertisement in a British paper was Helen Morrison, a spinster from Manchester. Her ad appeared in the *Manchester Weekly*

Journal in 1727. The mayor of Manchester took one look at it and committed her to a lunatic asylum for a month.

At sixty-two Mr Casey McGurr of Baltimore, Maryland, came across a lonely hearts advertisement from a woman describing herself as weighing eight stone four pounds and standing five feet four inches tall. They agreed to meet and in spite of discovering that the lady's true dimensions were nearer thirty-two stone and well over six feet, he proposed to her. Sadly the initial confusion led to later problems and the marriage was brief. Giving evidence at his divorce hearing Mr McGurr admitted: 'She proved too much for me when she grabbed the kettle and scalded me and then shot at me and then left me, saying I didn't appreciate a fat woman.'

Thirty-six-year-old Raymond Vanderzee of Boca Raton, Florida, was more fortunate. He advertised for a wife 'with big breasts and no stretch-marks'. He received eighteen replies to his ad and met up with each of the ladies in turn. All but one of the would-be Mrs Vanderzees agreed to sleep with Raymond on a trial basis and eventually he whittled his selection down to two front-runners. As he explained at the time of his divorce, 'I chose Suzy because her breasts were bigger, but it was a mistake. Angie has got smaller breasts, but I think we could be happy all the same. When my divorce from Suzy comes through, Angie and I plan to get married. Between now and then she's going to do a whole lot of exercises.'

Statistically less risky than advertising for a mate is to apply for one through a computer-dating agency. Following his divorce, Walter Davis added his name to a London computer dating service in the hope of finding himself a new partner. The computer searched its memory banks, went through thousands of prospective brides, and settled on one name – that of Ethel Davis, his former wife, who had signed up with the same service. Faced with such incontrovertible evidence of their compatibility, the couple decided to remarry.

Naturally ambitious go-getters don't need any help from computers or lonely hearts columns. When they want a partner they simply go out and grab. They don't always succeed, mark you...

At the turn of the century, the daughter of a Californian railway tycoon, determined to come home from Europe with a title, aimed her sights at an aristocratic young Englishman and pursued him relentlessly from London to his family seat in Yorkshire, where he finally popped the question.

All this time she had been detailing every move, ploy and stratagem in a stream of letters back home to her equally ambitious sister in San Francisco. The last, which carried the news of the final assault and victory, was on its way within twenty-four hours of the proposal.

A week later her sister's telegraphed reply arrived, coinciding disastrously with the engagement party thrown by the young man's mother. The butler carried it with the congratulatory telegrams to his young master who found himself reading aloud to the assembled company: MY OH MY YOU CLEVER LITTLE MINX STOP SO YOU CAUGHT YOUR BIG FISH AT LAST STOP THINKING FOLLOWING YOUR FOOTSTEPS SEE YOU SOON YOUR LADYSHIP.

Thus the coveted title slipped from her grasp at the eleventh hour.

The world over, everybody – well, almost everybody – wants to get married. In Britain ninety-three per cent of the adult population is married and although one in three marriages now ends in divorce, seventy per cent of divorcees remarry. What's more, according to a survey in *Wedding* magazine, ninety per cent of first-time marriers want a church wedding, not necessarily for religious reasons but because they find it 'reassuring'.

In fact, even at the altar disaster can strike. At a white wedding in Pennsylvania the couple were in the midst of taking their vows when the bridegroom collapsed. According to the clergyman conducting the service, the groom, 'fell to the floor as he uttered the binding words "I do". As I bent over him he whispered, "My God – I do", whereupon he died. The ceremony was over.'

The wife asked to be declared an 'official widow'.

Sixty years ago Albert Muldoon of Kileter, County Tyrone, attended a friend's wedding as best man. When the congregation rose to greet the bride, Albert unaccountably moved to the groom's left and stayed there throughout the service.

The priest naturally addressed his questions to the man standing next to the bride and Albert obediently gave his answers, including 'I do'. It was only during the signing of the register that the mistake came to light; the true groom insisted on signing as the husband although the priest had asked Albert to. A re-run of the ceremony followed immediately, this time with Albert standing in the right place.

Having seen his friend safely joined in wedlock. Albert commented, 'My pal Christopher, the bridegroom, was so nervous that he didn't seem able to speak, so I thought I had better answer for him.'

As someone once said, all marriages are happy. It's the living together afterwards that causes all the trouble.

On the wedding day itself most couples look on the bright side. In November 1979 Erik Estrada, the Puerto Rican star of the television cop series *Chips*, married his true love, Joyce Miller, and told waiting newsmen: 'I adore Joyce. Every man should have a woman like her. We are both very, very happy.' The bride echoed his feelings: 'Erik is the finest human being I know. There's so much happiness between us'; too much, it would seem, for them to manage.

Less than 300 days later (298 to be precise) Joyce filed for divorce. Her husband claimed that he had been 'enmeshed in a web of lies and fantasy Joyce created'. To which Joyce retorted, 'The lies started right from the beginning; the day we applied for the marriage licence. Living with Erik was the most bizarre experience of my life. I went through hell and it's a wonder that I kept my sanity.' The court was treated to a fuller exposition; Joyce submitted eighteen pages of evidence cataloguing her experiences – just over a page for every fortnight of her marriage.

Occasionally things go wrong before the newlyweds have even reached the honeymoon hotel. On their wedding day in 1956, Mr and Mrs Kenneth Marcle were driving away from the reception when their car got bogged down in sand near Holtville, California. It was clear that he would need help to shift the vehicle, so Mr Marcle left his wife and car and walked to the nearest town to fetch a breakdown truck. When he returned neither car nor wife were anywhere to be seen. They were reunited by chance the next day. Marcle ran into his wife in another town, where she casually announced that a stranger had freed the car after her husband had left and had taken her to Mexicali, Mexico, so they could both 'let their hair down'.

It was Oscar Wilde who described the Niagara Falls as 'the second biggest disappointment of the average American honeymoon'. So it certainly proved for Lorraine Templeton of Toronto, Canada, who stayed at the Love Hut Motel overlooking the Falls on her wedding night in 1976. At her divorce hearing she told the court, 'Lennie's friends had told me I shouldn't marry him. They even tied a sign saying "Lennie's a faggot" onto our car after the wedding, but I thought they were joking. When we got to the Motel I found out they were right. Lennie simply couldn't get it up. I was a virgin, but I still knew something was wrong somewhere.'

Wedding nights can go disastrously awry in a variety of ways . . . In the early 1920s London society was a little taken aback by the announcement that Sir Thomas Medlicott, until then one of the town's leading Lotharios, had decided to turn Romeo and take himself a wife. The lady in question was the breathtakingly beautiful American heiress Miss Gemma Franklin, many years his junior.

To the added amazement of one man in particular, the

Duke of Sutherland, Sir Thomas elected quite arbitrarily to spend his honeymoon at the Duke's magnificent highland home, Dunrobin, which was famous for its Gothic splendour and also for the second Duke's double-track private railway in the grounds. The Duke of Sutherland had never even met Sir Thomas, let alone invited him, but good breeding prevented him from raising any objections. After a delightful dinner at which the old knight's high spirits and rising colour belied his sixty-five years, the host suggested an early night. The suggestion was eagerly taken up by Sir Thomas, who escorted the new Lady Medlicott to bed with almost indecent haste.

The Duke of Sutherland was enjoying a nightcap a couple of hours later when her ladyship burst in on him in a state of some agitation. Her husband hadn't been seen since he went into the bathroom and she felt sure he was lost somewhere in the house.

Together they began to search the great salons and chambers and would have looked all over the castle if the sound of an engine whistle hadn't led them outside. All was made clear by the vision of Sir Thomas fulfilling a lifelong ambition as driver of the Dunrobin Express.

Rather more recently, a Mr Hans Mayer eagerly followed Elsa, his bride of a few hours, into their wedding bed and then ran into their first marital confrontation. Before allowing him to consummate their union Elsa set down a number of conditions which amounted to Hans agreeing that he would hand over his paypacket every week; that he would pay her £5 from his spending money every time they made love; and that he would never talk about his job as a gravedigger because it upset her. Their marriage got off to a nervous start.

Things got worse after the birth of their second child when Elsa doubled her charges. In the end Hans's spirit cracked and he took advantage of Elsa's young cousin whom he found taking a bath in their kitchen.

'It was very difficult for me,' he pleaded to the jury hearing his case. 'I couldn't save enough out of my spending money to pay her. I asked for credit but she refused to give me any. In nineteen years I could only afford to have her fifteen times. The strain was terrible.'

In the witness-box Elsa stood her ground, explaining, 'Nothing in life is free.'

In March 1971 Christine Brown married Ralph Smith and looked forward to a devoted lifetime together. The first night of the honeymoon brought its own surprises when Ralph joined his bride in bed with both arms bound up to the shoulders with sticking plaster. He mumbled some excuse, but his eager young bride playfully ripped the plaster from his arms to find them covered with tattoos, boldly proclaiming, 'True love to my dear wife Pam'.

His lack of foresight cost Ralph Smith £75 – £25 for the fine imposed for contracting a bigamous marriage and £50 to pay the doctor who removed the tattoos enabling him, in his own words, 'to make a clean start' with Christine.

Unfortunately, while most people seem keen to marry and some – like Henry VIII, Elizabeth Taylor and Mickey Rooney – seem keener than most, with many couples love turns to loathing all too soon.

The seventeenth-century English poet, John Dryden, endured a notoriously miserable marriage. His wife Elizabeth once complained to him that he spent far more time in his library than with her: 'Lord Mr Dryden! How can you always be poring over those musty books. I wish I were a book, and then I should have more of your company.'

'Pray, my dear,' he replied, 'if you do become a book let it be an almanack, for then I shall change you every year.'

Dryden really had no right to complain since he *chose* Elizabeth as his bride. Not everyone can choose whom they marry. For example, Queen Victoria's uncle, King George IV, had very mixed feelings about his official marriage to Princess Caroline of Brunswick. He met her for the first time with all due courtesy, kissed her hand gallantly, and then turned aside to one of his friends and said with an anguished whisper: 'For God's sake, George, give me a glass of brandy!'

Nowadays most people – including princes – can choose whom they marry, and having married them they can choose whether or not to remain true to their partners. As a rule, a goodly number of them don't. Like it or not, around the world infidelity is rife...

After picking up his fare an Athenian taxi-driver asked where the man wanted to go and was slightly taken aback to be given his own address. After dropping his passenger and being paid he watched with fascination as the man took out a key and let himself in through the door.

Using his own key the driver followed him and interrupted the man's secret liaison with his wife.

'It must have been his unlucky day,' said the driver philosophically. 'Athens has 70,000 taxis.'

Elaine Shaw of Brisbane had a nasty shock when she sent a specimen of her boyfriend's handwriting to a calligraphy expert who had been advertising in the local press, offering to tell fortunes for a modest fee.

'Please find enclosed an example of my boyfriend's writing,' she wrote in her covering letter. 'Can you tell me if he would make a good husband?'

'No, I'm afraid he won't, my dear,' replied the graphologist by return post. 'He's been a pretty rotten one to me for the last three years. But thanks for the evidence.'

The friendship between an Austrian taxi-driver and a landscape painter came to an untimely end when the taxi-driver discovered one of his friend's creations adorning his own wife's bottom. The artist and the lady were in bed one evening at the artist's studio. The lady was watching *Gone With The Wind* on television. The artist wasn't interested in love stories, so he started doodling on her bottom with a felt-tip pen and completed a rather pleasing landscape before dropping off to sleep. When he awoke his love had gone.

Back home she slipped between her own sheets just before her husband got in from his night-shift driving round Vienna.

'I thought I would give her a goodnight kiss,' he told the court hearing his divorce petition. 'It was then I saw the landscape – signed with Johann's name. It was his signature, and to prove it, I woke my wife up and we compared it to another signature on a painting he gave us that hangs in the dining-room.'

It was Groucho Marx who observed that 'behind every great man is a woman. And behind her is his wife.' And when that wife discovers what her husband has been up to, *anything* can happen.

One morning Antonio Laina woke up in his Naples home to find his jealous wife cutting off his nose with a pair of scissors.

The discovery of her husband's adultery dealt a crushing blow to Vera Czermak of Prague. With her life in ruins she saw death as a welcome relief and launched herself into its arms from her third-floor balcony. As luck and Nemesis would have it her husband was walking directly underneath at the time. Mrs Czermak landed right on top of him, killing him outright. She escaped with only minor injuries.

Just once in a while it's the man who manages to have the last word. Among the bequests in the will of a Philadelphia industrialist who died in 1947 was one that read: 'To my wife I leave her lover, and the knowledge that I wasn't the fool she thought I was.'

ROUGH AND TUMBLE

'Sex and violence came into Jane
Morgan's life gradually. Then she
became a Christian and matters
escalated.'

Essex County Standard

'Gentlemen, this is War! First reports say the Japanese
have raped Shirley Temple.'

A young bride-to-be wrote recently to the magazine *Woman's Own*: 'I am engaged to a wonderful man, but lately he has been very moody and is always hitting me. He says it is nothing to what I shall get after marriage, and I must get used to being kept under control. Please advise me: I want to marry him, but I don't know how to handle the situation.'

It's not easy when the slap and tickle get out of hand...

Passing judgement in a case of wife-beating a British magistrate told the court that he thought there were times when it was proper for a man to beat his wife, since holy scripture supported it. Such beatings should only be given as a service of love, he added, not in a fit of temper. In the case in question, however, he regretted that instead of employing a reasonably sized stick the accused had lost his temper and had set about his wife with an iron bar.

Naturally, everybody's different and some are better equipped than others to take the rough and tumble of married life in their stride.

When a Glasgow woman, who had already told a Sheriff's court that her husband was used to burning her with cigarettes and beating her up, was asked whether she regarded theirs as a happy marriage, she answered without hesitation: 'Oh, yes.'

And in some relationships there seems to be a positive lust for violence. After his wife had wrecked two of their cars following rows with him, Dallas Sherman divorced her. He later repented and they were remarried. But their second attempt at wedded bliss was even less harmonious than the first, and after Irene had shot Dallas in the chest and once in the hand he divorced her a second time. Irene shot Dallas a third time during efforts to patch up their relationship, but, as on the previous occasions, Dallas pulled through and, in 1977, married Irene for a third and final time.

Of course it is well known that television can bring violence into the home. The controversy over who shot 'J.R.' in the TV series *Dallas* culminated in a true-life domestic tragedy for one real Dallas household. The couple involved argued over the identity of the unknown assailant in the television series with such ferocity that during one of the commercial breaks the wife fetched the family shotgun and put an end to the squabble by killing her husband. It was never revealed which of them had been right.

If having a television can lead to disaster, so can being without one. When French police charged Louis Pilar of Rheims with shooting and wounding his wife he blamed a three-week television strike, saying: 'There was nothing to look at and I was bored.' His wife backed him up and told detectives who visited her in hospital: 'I don't blame my husband. It really has been boring in the evenings.'

People in love can have shocking problems. Witness this letter sent to the magazine *Woman's Mirror*: 'I suffer so much from static electricity in my clothes and on me that when I kiss my boyfriend I give him violent electric shocks. My boyfriend is beginning to think it's not worth it.'

How like a man! When Robert Richardson of Ashland, Oregon, wired up his girlfriend Rita's breasts to give her 'exciting little electric shocks' she raised no objections, but when Rita attempted to return the compliment by wiring up Robert's penis he took her to court, claiming damages of $100,000 for the 'impairment of his manhood'. He explained to the court, 'I knew what I was doing to Rita because the wiring came from my old train set. She shouldn't have touched me with the wires. She has no understanding of voltage.' He lost the case.

A sixty-three-year-old Brazilian who was so overcome by the sight of a girl in a mini-skirt sitting next to him on a bus that he bit her thigh was sent to jail for three days in Belo Horizonte. After hearing his sentence the man told reporters: 'The Pope was right. Mini-skirts are dangerous.'

The long-running affair between a couple in Akron, Ohio, came to an abrupt end when the bride-to-be shot her future husband in the leg and he called off the wedding. As it turned out this was just the most recent in a succession of similar shootings. The lady had shot at her fiancé on thirty-three separate occasions, though this last was the only one he had reported to the police.

In court the lady was unrepentant. She explained that she was a crack shot and when she fired she 'only inflicted minor .22 flesh wounds – and then only if we have a real flare-up'.

Following a lovers' tiff a Parisian threw his girlfriend from the fourth-floor window of his apartment. On her way to the pavement she landed in an awning that broke her fall and then she slid to the ground feet first. Immediately she dashed back up the stairs, took her boyfriend by surprise and knocked him silly with a bottle of wine.

When Roy Barton married his wife Tina he did so in the full knowledge that thirty-three years earlier her mother had caused a sensation in New Zealand by stabbing her father to death. What Roy didn't know at the time of his marriage was that Tina was unable to have children. In their place she littered the house with dolls and pets; but they were a poor substitute. She and Roy started to have rows which reached their peak on April Fool's Day 1977. After calling her 'a childless bitch' and 'the daughter of a whore and a murderess' he dared Tina to do to him what her mother had done to her father, adding somewhat illogically that she wouldn't be able to because he came from Invercargill, the world's most southerly city according to Barton, 'and you can't kill an Invercargill man!'

Tina Barton proved the flaw in his argument by stabbing her husband thirty-six times. She went into the same Christchurch dock as her mother had done, but fared better. The jury only found her guilty of manslaughter.

Some years ago the *Daily Herald* reported the case of a man who called his doctor in to treat him for a bad case of 'flu. As the doctor was leaving the patient saw him kiss his wife at the bottom of the stairs. 'The husband,' in the paper's words, ' "under great provocation" nearly hit the doctor with a milk bottle, but out of respect for the doctor's profession he refrained, and punched his wife instead.'

A thirty-seven-year-old West German woman from Oldenburg disapproved so vehemently of her husband's heavy drinking that one day when she found him slumped motionless over the kitchen table she lost her head and shot him twice.

At her trial she was found guilty, though the evidence revealed the murder to be a disastrous case of overkill. The husband had in fact died of a heart attack shortly before she shot him.

'Kissing don't last', wrote George Meredith, 'cookery do!'

This seems to have been the philosophy of Nick Papas of Los Angeles who refused to kiss his common-law wife, Mary Smith, while continuing to eat meals prepared by her. Mary didn't take kindly to forgoing her customary goodnight peck and stabbed Nick to death with a butcher's knife.

A South African hang-glider, James Barthes, spotted a woman sun-bathing in the nude on her rooftop and was so overcome that he made an obscene gesture at her as he flew overhead. The lady's husband, who had seen the air-to-ground signal from the bedroom, grabbed his submachine gun and brought Barthes down in a hail of bullets.

A thirty-year-old Thai woman from Bangkok who found out that her husband was having an affair with a neighbour, attacked him before dawn one day and cut off his penis with a razor. Pausing only to wrap the severed member in paper she set off with it by bus to a town 650 kilometres from the capital.

The husband was rushed to hospital where he underwent emergency treatment and was said to be in a fair condition, though surgeons declined to speculate whether they could reunite him with his manhood once his wife had been arrested.

Worried neighbours called the police to a Glasgow house where the officers found a man attacking his wife with an axe. When arrested and cautioned the man's only comments were: 'I should have killed her and got it done with. Anyway did you hear how the Celtic got on?'

The tension brought on by hearing the details of their legal separation proved too much for a Florida couple who got into a violent row in the judge's chamber, pulled guns on each other and started a gunfight across the room.

This was brought to a swift end by a witness in the neighbouring courtroom, who borrowed a gun from the presiding judge, broke into the scene of the fighting and shot both husband and wife.

Not all marriages that come to a violent end are unhappy, of course. Police who broke into the home of a recently married couple in Suresnes near Paris found the young lovers lying dead in their bedroom. Germaine Liebaut was wearing her wedding dress, her husband Albert lay beside her. Detectives established that she had shot Albert before turning the gun on herself. The rest of the mystery was answered by the note found with them which read:

'We are killing ourselves because we are too happy . . . we do not need money, for we are worth over 30,000 francs. We have good health and a wonderful future before us, but we prefer to die now because we are the happiest people in the world. We adore each other but would rather descend into the grave together while we are still so happy.'

COURTROOM DRAMA

'It ain't no sin if you crack a few laws now and then, just so long as you don't break any.'

Mae West

'We understand your husband *was* a swine, Mrs Bascomb, but did you have to barbecue him?'

For serious students of sexual disasters there's no place like a court of law. All human life is there...

In 1979 in Houston, Texas, Ms Cindy Lamont took her hairdresser to court after he had accidentally dyed her pubic hair green. 'My fiancé thought I was a natural red-head,' she explained, 'but when he saw that my pubic hair had turned green he became suspicious. When I admitted that I was really a brunette he called off our engagement. He is a very rich man and because of the incompetence of my hairdresser I have lost a fortune.'

The court offered Ms Lamont its condolences and ordered the hairdresser to pay her costs and compensation of $25 – the price of a pubic shampoo and rinse.

In 1972 in Düsseldorf, West Germany, Karl and Renate Maass successfully sued the young couple who lived in the apartment above theirs. Herr and Frau Maass were in their mid-sixties and told the court they only made love about ten times a year, which they considered quite normal for people of their age. Their neighbours however were in their twenties and, by their own admission, made love at least ten times a week. The Maasses had no objection to this, in principle. What disturbed them was the noise made by the young lovers during their love-making. Apparently the young man yodelled while his girlfriend screamed hysterically. Herr and Frau Maass had frequently asked them to make less noise, but their requests were ignored and when the plaster on the ceiling of their bedroom began to crumble during one of the youngsters' more passionate nights, the elderly couple decided they had no alternative but to start legal proceedings.

The court ordered the young couple to pay for the damage caused to the Maasses' ceiling by their exertions and instructed them either to make love in silence in future or to move to a different apartment, preferably one on the ground floor.

An eighteen-year-old nursery nurse from Deal, Kent, was found guilty of indecent exposure and fined £10 after she admitted travelling topless on a train from Ashford to Folkestone on a Sunday morning. Her boyfriend and his brother had been with her at the time and found her behaviour quite acceptable. However, the fourth passenger in the carriage objected and made a formal complaint to the guard.

A fifty-five-year-old woman who fell off a chair while playing bingo was awarded £10,000 damages for the loss of her sex-life. Her husband was given £50 for the loss of consortium.

Having heard counsel for the plaintiff arguing that his twenty-five-year-old client's sex life had been affected by an accident with a bulldozer, the judge asked if the man was married. When counsel replied that he wasn't, the judge observed, 'Well, I cannot see how it affects his sex life.'

Before going to meet her new boyfriend, Ermis, Mlle Claudine Tousel, a French bank cashier from Alençon, took advantage of the ready supply of paper money at work to compensate for what she saw as a natural disadvantage: her flat chest. 'I know men like women with big ones, so I filled up my bra with notes,' she told the court hearing the charge of theft brought against her. Unfortunately her encounter with Ermis was not a great success: 'Ermis was fondling me behind the bank when he suddenly remembered an important engagement. I never saw him again.' Mlle Tousel had meant to return the banknotes, but in her distress at losing her lover she quite forgot. Verdict: Guilty.

Robert La Vega, a self-styled 'sex enthusiast' of Key Biscayne, Florida, was taken to court and charged with defacing public property. Over a period of three years, between 1977 and 1980, he had borrowed a total of over two hundred different books from the public library and had systematically defaced the title pages of every one. He pleaded Not Guilty saying that far from defacing the books he had 'enhanced their value with joyous life-affirming statements'. Examples of his graffiti included:

THE WORD FOR THE DAY IS LEGS – SPREAD THE WORD!

BE NICE TO BOOBS: THEY OUTNUMBER PEOPLE TWO TO ONE.

LIBRARIANS MAKE NOVEL LOVERS.

THE SECOND GREATEST SIN IN THE WORLD IS TO TURN AWAY FROM YOUR LOVER WHEN YOU KNOW THEY WANT SEX. THE GREATEST SIN IN THE WORLD IS TO HAVE SEX WHEN YOU DON'T WANT IT.

THE MOST BEAUTIFUL GIRL IN THE WORLD HAS GOT SPOTS ON HER ASS.

IF YOU'RE FEELING HORNY, SMILE AT THE LIBRARIAN.

ALL LOLLIPOPS DON'T HAVE THE SAME FLAVOR.

FUCK JANE AUSTEN.

Observing that not all Mr La Vega's statements were of

equal literary merit, the judge found him guilty and fined him $2,000.

To Mrs Patrick Campbell marriage represented 'the deep, deep peace of the double-bed after the hurly-burly of the chaise-longue'. It was a little bit like that for Mrs Caroline Manders of Leeds, but while Mrs C found the nuptial quiet life a positive relief, Mrs M didn't like it one bit. Through-out her eighteen-month engagement to Rory Manders, Caroline and her fiancé enjoyed what she described as 'a very active and varied sex life together'. Come the wedding day, however, Rory suddenly lost interest in sex. Prior to their marriage the couple had made love at least four times a week. Once they were man and wife, they made love hardly at all. 'Being married took all the fun out of it,' according to Rory, who as a bachelor had slept in the nude but as a married man took to wearing pyjamas and playing Solitaire in bed. 'For the first year of our marriage we had sex only once,' Caroline told the court hearing her divorce petition. 'During the next two years we didn't have sex at all and finally, when I made a scene about it and threatened to tell Rory's mother, he promised always to have sex with me on my birthday.'

Caroline was granted her divorce. She was born in 1952 – on 29 February.

As a follow-up to a highly successful re-modelling job on a patient's breasts, an American plastic surgeon suggested she might benefit from a re-alignment of her navel. The lady agreed and the operation went ahead, but when the dress-ings were removed she was far from satisfied.

'In the first place it is eight inches above the site of my old navel,' she complained. 'Mr Dearing assured me that the navel he intended to create would resemble a small walnut. I have finished up with something more like a coconut.'

In his defence the surgeon said that he had done what he could to achieve the walnut effect but the patient's tissues hadn't been top quality material. He said that he had tried to make amends by offering to marry her but this had been declined.

In Britain some years ago, long before the reform of the divorce laws, a man accused of bigamy appeared before Mr Justice Maule. When asked if he had anything to say in his defence the poor fellow explained that his wife had run off with a hawker five years earlier. As he hadn't seen her since, he had married his second wife without going through the accepted divorce procedures, which were anyway quite beyond his means.

The judge addressed him sternly: 'Prisoner at the Bar, I will tell you what you ought to have done, and if you say you did not know, I will tell you that the Law conclusively presumes that you did. You ought to have instructed your attorney to bring an action against the hawker for criminal conversation with your wife. That would have cost you about £100. When you had recovered substantial damages against the hawker, you would have instructed your attorney to sue in the ecclesiastical courts for a divorce *a mensa atque thoro*. That would have cost you £200 or £300 more. When you had obtained a divorce *a mensa atque thoro*, you would have had to appear by counsel before the House of Lords for a divorce *a vinculo matrimonii*. The Bill might have been opposed in all its stages in both Houses of Parliament, and altogether you would have had to spend about £1,000 or £1,200. You will probably tell me that you never had 1,000 farthings of your own in the world, but, prisoner, that makes no difference. Sitting here as a British judge, it is my duty to tell you that this is not a country in which there is one law for the rich and another for the poor.'

At 3 o'clock one morning a police patrol car in London noticed two men, a woman, and a dog walking along the pavement. One of the men was carrying a ladder, a torch and a camera, and the police stopped them to ask why. After a whispered conversation their reason was given and they were allowed to continue.

A few doors away they stopped outside a house, placed the ladder against the sill of a first-floor window and held it steady while the man with the torch and camera climbed up, opened the window and went into the room.

'He's here!' he shouted with a note of triumph, shining the torch on a couple he had found in bed and taking a photograph of them – proof he hoped of his wife's adultery.

He took the case to court where the judge asked if he could have a look at the photograph. Here the man's case started to disintegrate: 'I was so excited I forgot to take off the lens-cap,' he confessed.

When his wife went into the witness-box she explained that the man in bed with her had recently had all his teeth removed and that she had just made him a bowl of soup.

Allen Farber of Chicago divorced his wife after she had denied him access to her bed. He then sued his former in-laws because his ex-wife's mother had warned her not to have any children by him in case they were born with their father's looks.

A man from West Surrey who applied to a local court for a divorce later withdrew 'in case his wife got to hear about it'.

'Women,' said W. C. Fields, 'are like elephants to me: I like to look at them, but I wouldn't want to own one.'

Walter Randall, a cabaret and circus entertainer from New Orleans, was happy to own both. His marriage ended in divorce, however, because his wife refused to make love inside the elephant's cage. For Walter to perform with his wife in front of their baby elephant Zuleta was quite a turn-on. Mrs Randall found it otherwise. 'The stench was terrible,' she said, 'and I didn't want Zuleta to see me like that. It's not natural.'

The largest number of people known to have appeared stark naked in a courtroom at the same time is sixteen. One Saturday night during the summer of 1966 sixteen young men and women – their ages ranging from seventeen to nineteen – were spotted by police dancing in the nude in a street in Brooklyn, New York. They were arrested and taken immediately to the police court to be charged with indecency. When the court heard that the sixteen had been attending a High School graduation party, the judge released them on condition that they were each driven to their parents' home exactly as they appeared in court – dressed only in a blanket.

Barely a couple of months after being bound over to keep the peace, George McPhee, from Islington in London, described as a poet, was arrested in his flat for screaming.

When taken to court he told the magistrates that he had 'had a bad day' and went on to elaborate: 'Browsing in Harrod's book department, I earmarked a copy of Fulke Greville's *Collected Works*, went to have a quick look at the Children's Bookshelf, and when I got back an Arab had snapped up the Greville.

'Then I went for a drink with a social worker who consumed twenty-eight glasses of beer and, having invited her home, I found I could not get rid of her. So I began to scream.'

The police who went to the flat questioned the social worker about her reasons for refusing to leave and were told that she was Mrs McPhee.

A Bolton woman petitioning for a divorce was asked to give an example of her husband's behaviour.

'Last year Harry asked me if I had anything to discuss before the football season began,' she said.

In 1981 an Irishman living in Shepherd's Bush, London, appeared in court charged with assaulting a twenty-five-year-old secretary in Holland Park. He pleaded Not Guilty and maintained that the girl had been not only willing but eager for his advances. Counsel for the prosecution denied this and said it was a clear case of assault.

'If it was,' called out the defendant with a grin, 'it was assault with a friendly weapon.'

'What do you mean by that?' asked counsel sarcastically.

'This!' said the defendant as he dramatically exposed himself in court.

'Put that away or I'll put you away,' thundered the judge.
'I won't,' said the man.
'I will,' said the judge.
And he did.

In 1979 a Brisbane court heard from one of the city's traffic policemen of how he had been 'patrolling Redcliffe Parade when I saw the accused driving a souped-up wheelchair in an erratic manner. I signalled him to stop but he revved up and began to weave in and out of the street furniture. Finally he went out of control and crashed into Standyman's Funeral Parlour.'

The driver pleaded guilty to being drunk in charge of a wheelchair, but told the court: 'I had been visiting my ex-wife. We had our customary scene and I wanted to get away from her as quickly as possible.'

A few years ago Constable Phiri was on duty in his police station in Ndola, Zambia, when a twenty-six-year-old woman came in to report a man who had threatened her with a gun. Constable Phiri took her statement – and then offered her ten shillings to go to bed with him. She refused. The offer was increased to fifty shillings and the lady and the policeman made their way upstairs, where, in the station's lecture-room, Phiri stripped off all his clothes and invited his new friend to do the same.

Their dealings were still in progress when the lecture-room door opened and Assistant Commissioner Humphrey Nthere of the Zambian CID led in a class of trainee detectives for a formal lesson on police procedure. Seeing Constable Phiri, he explained to him that irregular conduct was not allowed in the lecture-room, but Phiri replied that he was busy taking a statement and asked the Assistant Commissioner and his pupils to leave him alone for a few minutes more.

Inevitably the superior officer had the last word and Phiri found himself taken in front of the magistrate who asked him to account for his action. 'So far as I know there is no rule against fornication in the station,' Phiri protested. 'I paid to satisfy my desires, and I removed my uniform out of respect.'

A woman giving evidence about the state of her marriage told Tottenham police court: 'My husband is a jolly good sort, one of those very hearty men. He wears plus-fours, smokes a pipe, and talks about nothing but beer and rugby football. My nerves won't stand much more of it.'

While empanelling a jury in his court in Santa Cruz, California, the judge dismissed one of the jurors, saying: 'This woman is my wife. She never pays any attention to what I say at home and I have no reason to believe that her behaviour in court would be any different.'

A British Divorce Court awarded Mrs Joan Wallace a divorce on the grounds of cruelty after hearing what the judge, Mr Justice Cumming-Bruce, had described as her husband's 'lamentable and wanton lack of consideration'.

During the hearing the court had been treated to details of some of Mr Wallace's more bizarre exploits. Like many husbands faced with their wives' first pregnancy he showed great concern for her well-being and that of the baby, but his solicitude went beyond the normal bounds when he became obsessed by calcium deficiency and insisted that she ate bonemeal fertilizer.

The next bee in his bonnet was her engagement ring; he didn't think she took adequate care of it. So one day when he found it lying about in the house he slipped it over one of his toes and waited to see what happened. Mrs Wallace, who had deliberately removed the ring during her housework, assumed she had lost it and realized her husband would be livid. It was some time before she saw the ring again because her husband took to wearing two pairs of socks and only removed one pair before getting into bed. Only when she persuaded him to take off the inner pair for darning and a long overdue wash did the ring come to light.

Dr Max Feldman, a New York dentist, suggested to one of his female patients that he gave her an anaesthetic before proceeding to remove one of her teeth. Misconstruing his intentions, the patient grabbed the dentist's testicles and held them in a vice-like grip.

Dr Feldman took the case to court, but the patient emerged triumphant with an award of $500. Unfortunately, in the panic to free himself from her grip, the dentist had broken one of the patient's fingers.

A Canadian couple calling themselves Mr and Mrs John Smith were taken to court by a hotel in Vancouver because of a dispute over an unpaid bill. The couple had booked for one night at the cost of $78. When the room service waiter came into the room with the couple's breakfast, he found four other couples also there and a ten-person orgy in full swing. The waiter reported his discovery to the hotel manager who added an extra $312 to the Smiths' bill. Mr Smith refused to pay, saying that he and his wife had booked a Family Room and the price for that was just $78. Since the hotel had not stipulated how many people could occupy a Family Room, the court found in favour of the Smiths.

During a New York rape trial the victim went into the witness-box and was asked under cross-examination what the accused had said to her. 'I couldn't possibly repeat it, your honour,' she said. The judge smiled benignly and told her to write it on a piece of paper. This was duly passed along the jury where it came to a halt at one of the lady jurors who had nodded off after a good lunch. Her male neighbour gave her a gentle nudge and slipped the paper into her hand, 'I'm going to fuck you like you've never been fucked before,' read the astonished female juror, who promptly turned round and slapped her colleague's face.

When passing judgement in a case in which a wife had thrown 'almost every form of domestic utensil' at her husband, Mr Justice Karminski concluded that she could not be considered cruel since on almost every occasion she had missed.

You know the apocryphal story of the lawyer who couldn't remember the difference between arson and incest – and set fire to his sister. The disaster that befell Johann Huber was as dramatic – and much sadder, because Herr Huber's story is true.

Huber was a much-married Munich man who belonged to that sorry band who suffer from bed problems – not so much problems in bed as those caused by the bed itself. As he explained to the court hearing a charge of arson against him:

'After I found my first wife in bed with the milkman, my second with the postman, and my third with the chimney-sweep, I came to the conclusion that the cause of the trouble lay with my bed. There was something wrong with it. As I dislike acting hastily I decided to have another go before getting rid of it – so I married Martha. She was a perfect wife. She made me forget everything. The trouble was her mother.

'On the first night she slept in the bed with Martha. I had to use the divan. Next morning she presented me with a set of rules saying when I could and couldn't make love. It was too much. I was only in bed once a month. The rest of the time her mother, and at the weekends her mother's friends, slept in it.'

Herr Huber endured this for a year, but after a bleak dozen nights in the bed he had had enough and put a match to it. This was an ill-judged action. Flames from the bed ignited his neighbour's house and razed it to the ground. The bill for the damage was £42,000 and poor Herr Huber went to prison for two years.

In the course of an assault case the judge asked the victim why she had removed her petticoat in the accused's car on the night of the incident. 'It was rather an expensive one,' she explained, 'and I knew what he was going to do but I was so frightened I couldn't stop him. I asked him if I could take it off as I did not want to get it crumpled.'

A New York husband who got his own back on his divorced wife by writing 'adultress' after her name on alimony cheques was ordered to stop by a judge who ruled: 'No woman should be put in the position of publishing a libel against herself in order to cash a cheque to which she is entitled.'

What is adultery? You know and I know – at least in theory we do – but not everyone is as well informed on the subject as we are. Defendants in divorce cases, when asked if they know the meaning of adultery, have occasionally offered some highly original definitions:

- 'I thought it meant drinking with men in public houses.'
- 'I didn't think it was adultery during the daytime.'
- 'I thought it meant getting a girl into trouble.'
- 'Adultery is having sexual intercourse with a woman not your wife, who is not over fifty years of age; and it is not adultery if she is over fifty.'

George Burns defined adultery – though not in court, needless to say – as 'doing in the day with somebody else's wife what you do in the night with your own'.

In court and on oath, another Hollywood actor, James Sanders, said, 'It's called adultery because adults do it, but it's pretty juvenile.' Sanders had good cause to feel that way about it. He was in bed with the wife of a friend one night when the friend came home unexpectedly. Hearing the husband climbing the stairs, Sanders quickly hid himself in the closet where he remained all night. In the morning the friend opened the closet door to find Sanders naked and fast asleep on the closet floor.

Twenty-six years of marriage ended for Doris and Albert May when a divorce court judge ruled that their differences were irreconcilable. According to Doris, Albert used to run around naked playing a tambourine outside their house whenever she refused him sex, and Albert claimed that she charged £4 every time she granted him connubial rights.

A German wife who told a court in Dortmund that she and her husband had not made love for at least eighteen months was astonished to hear him shout, 'It's a lie! We made love on the floor of my office yesterday morning!'

'He's the one who is lying,' shouted back his wife.

However, the husband had the last word. 'I can prove it,' he said triumphantly. 'I marked her arse with the office date-stamp.'

A man whose wife insisted that he kissed her, then her sister, and then the cat when he came home from work was granted a divorce by the judge who ruled that the wife had adopted a very unreasonable attitude.

It's not only humans whose sex lives can take them to court. It happens to animals as well. Sicilian pet-owner Franco Boretti was given two fines of 67p each after his dog had been found guilty of committing 'an obscene act in a public place'.

On the steps of the courthouse he told the world: 'I resent Blackie being branded as a playdog by the gutter press.

'It is quite true that he had the pharmacist's poodle bitch twice in fifteen minutes on the steps of the Convent of St Mary, but he has had almost every bitch in Porto Venus over the past three years. I don't see what is so special about a mangy poodle.'

Asked about his relationship with the owner of the ravaged poodle, Signor Boretti acknowledged that their friendship had come to an end. 'We had played dominoes together for close on sixty years. What does he expect me to do? Show Blackie the two fine tickets? As for having my animal fixed – I would rather go to Russia.'

In San Francisco, California, in 1969 a young woman was arrested and charged with soliciting because she was found walking the streets wearing a tee-shirt that bore the legend PUSSY FOR SALE on the front and SIT ON A HAPPY FACE on the back. When she appeared at the police court to be charged she was wearing another tee-shirt. It read: BEAT ME, BITE ME, WHIP ME, FUCK ME. COME ALL OVER MY TITS AND TELL ME THAT YOU LOVE ME BABY. THEN GET THE FUCK OUT.

The case was dismissed and she was discharged after she had explained to the court that she wasn't a prostitute, but a model on her way to a photographic assignment.

WHY CAN'T A WOMAN
BE MORE LIKE A MAN?

'I'm a practising heterosexual – but
bi-sexuality immediately doubles your
chances for a date on Saturday night.'

Woody Allen

'D'you know what I miss most since I've become
Claudette? Darts.'

When, in the 1940s, a notorious homosexual Member of the House of Commons announced his engagement, Winston Churchill was shown a newspaper photograph of the MP and his remarkably plain bride-to-be. 'Ah well,' said Churchill, 'buggers can't be choosers.'

Genuine bisexuals, on the other hand, are spoilt for choice. And reliable research suggests that most buggers *are* bisexual. In the West it seems that only one person in twenty is exclusively homosexual, while over twenty per cent of the population is ready and willing to get the best of both worlds. What's more, surveys of American gays indicate that fifty-three per cent of male homosexuals have had intercourse with a woman and seventy-five per cent of lesbians have had sex with a man.

The fact is that bisexuals, from Alexander the Great to Billie Jean King, have sex lives that are undeniably more varied than those of committed homo- or heterosexuals. The consolation is that their sex lives are as disaster-prone as anybody else's.

Literary history is littered with the names of distinguished authors who were – in Noel Coward's immortal phrase – 'Tommy Two-ways', but few writers can have been as versatile as Lord Byron, Algernon Swinburne and Truman Capote.

In the course of his short life (1788–1824) Byron had sex with young boys, young girls and more than three hundred grown women, including his nanny and his sister. To be fair, he was only nine years old when he was at it with his nanny, the boys were school friends at Harrow, and his sister was only his half-sister – and she was married at the time. Her name was Augusta Leigh and she and Byron shared a father, and a daughter, and, by all accounts, a lot of laughs.

Swinburne, by contrast, lived longer (1837–1909) but

was less of a family man. He never had sex with his relations, but he regularly had relations with a monkey. Apart from bestiality, his chief enthusiasms were for being beaten and for sleeping with young boys, and he only managed one fully fledged affair with a mature woman. It was not a success. At its height Swinburne's middle-aged paramour was heard to complain, 'I can't seem to make him understand that biting's no good.'

Any list of sexually versatile contemporary writers has to include Truman Capote, who by his own admission was 'a beautiful little boy ... and everybody had me – men, women, dogs and fire hydrants. I did it with everybody. I didn't slow down until I was nineteen, and then I became very circumspect.'

One of Lord Byron's many mistresses was Lady Caroline Lamb, whose long-suffering husband William went on to become Lord Melbourne and British Prime Minister. Caroline made a habit of sending her boyfriends locks of her pubic hair, though in snipping off a modest tress for Byron the scissors slipped and she cut herself. Byron reciprocated with an intimate kiss-curl of his own, but handled the scissors more adroitly.

Despite Lord Byron and Caroline Lamb, pubic hair was not a subject much discussed in high society in the early part of the nineteenth century. It took one hundred and fifty years and the advent of Mary Quant for pubic hairstyles to become the talk of the town. In 1970, having given her own pubic hair an endearing heartshape, trend-setting Miss Quant told an expectant world: 'We shall move towards exposure and body cosmetics and certainly pubic hair will become a fashion emphasis, if not necessarily blatant.'

Taking his cue from Quant, a fashion-conscious London journalist called Harry asked his girlfriend if he could trim her pubic hair so that it represented the letter H. She was strangely reluctant, but he pressed her and eventually, as a Valentine's Day treat for him, she agreed. The reason for her reluctance was that Harry was not her only lover. She also shared a flat – and her bed – with a girl called Sheila who knew nothing of Harry until the disastrous night when poor Sheila found herself face to face with an immaculately tonsured H.

Of all the fine writers of the past century who were either homosexual or who fancied both men and women – Gide, Genet, Auden, Isherwood, Whitman, Wilder, Forster, Maugham, Rimbaud, Verlaine, Proust, Tennessee Williams, Angus Wilson, etc. – the most celebrated and the most tragic must be Oscar Wilde. His brother William said of him, 'Oscar is a perfect gentleman. You can trust him with a lady anywhere.'

The Oscar Wilde story is certainly a great sexual disaster, but really too serious and sad to belong in this collection. As his wife observed, 'I think his fate is rather like Humpty Dumpty's, quite as tragic and quite as impossible to put right.'

Algernon Swinburne wrote a cruel epitaph for Wilde:

> When Oscar came to join his God,
> Not earth to earth but sod to sod,
> It was for sinners such as this
> Hell was created bottomless.

Although Wilde went with women, he much preferred boys. After he had been released from prison and was living in exile in France he was persuaded against his instincts and his better judgement to have a final fling with a female prostitute. He was taken to a brothel in Dieppe and when he emerged was asked for his verdict: 'The first these ten years, and it will be the last,' he said. 'It was like cold mutton. But tell it in England, for it will entirely restore my character.'

In London in the 1970s a bisexual author, husband and father fell head over heels in love with a young man to whom he gave the nickname Bo-bo. In a passionate but ill-considered moment the author promised to dedicate his next book to the youth. He sent the manuscript to the publishers with the inscription 'To my darling Bo-bo' and thought no more about it until a few weeks before publication when he started to panic about what his wife and children might think. To avert disaster and keep everybody happy, he started to call his wife Bo-bo as well.

When Elton John got married in Australia on Valentine's Day, 1984 he emerged from the church with his bride on his arm to be greeted by the world's press and an enthusiastic crowd of well-wishers, one of whom called cheerily to the newly-wed Elton, 'Good on yer, poofter!'

At an English wedding in 1983 one of the guests made a remark that was less well-intentioned. As the bride and groom walked down the aisle at the end of the service, the guest – a thirty-six-year-old merchant banker from Gerrards Cross – turned to his neighbour and said in an audible stage whisper, 'I've had them both. They're useless.'

On 17 July 1969, his tenth wedding anniversary, John Rollins of San Diego, California, left his wife Shirley and moved in with his chauffeur, a six-foot-four-inch-tall black man called Harry. They were lying on the sun roof in the apartment block where Harry lived, holding hands and feeling free, when a plane flew overhead. Attached to the tail

of the plane was a fluttering banner which bore the words 'I LOVE YOU SHIRLEY – JOHN'. John had ordered the flying message three months before as an anniversary surprise for his wife. In the event, it was Harry who got the surprise and John who got the shock. Harry, roused by the airborne declaration, turned on his lover, hit him in the face and broke two of his ribs. Neighbours, hearing the rooftop screams, called the police. Harry was arrested, charged and eventually imprisoned. John went back to his wife.

At Luton Juvenile Court recently a psychologist, asked to speak on behalf of a sixteen-year-old defendant accused of two offences against girls, could only say: 'Previously he has been found guilty of offences which suggested a homosexual nature. These latest offences are at least a step in the right direction.'

In 1798 the threat of invasion by Napoleon's forces from across the Channel had only recently subsided when the Bishop of Durham rose to his feet in the House of Lords and warned the nation that the only reason the French had given up the idea of a military conquest was to concentrate their energies on destroying the *moral* foundations of British society by smuggling in hordes of ballet dancers.

Nowadays even the clergy accept that not all male ballet dancers are homosexual. Waslwa Nijinsky, probably the most famous ballet dancer of them all, was definitely bisexual. He found having sex at all something of a burden, and his partners found it something of a disappointment. By all accounts he had a minute libido and equipment to match.

In 1978 in Boston disaster struck another poorly endowed ballet dancer during the première of a new ballet.

Feeling self-conscious about his appearance the dancer decided to pad out his jock strap with tissue paper. It felt comfortable and he sensed it looked good – at least it did when he first came on stage. Unfortunately as the performance progressed the tissue paper became dislodged and gradually moved away from the dancer's crutch and down his leg. By the time he came to take his curtain call he appeared to have grown a vast goitre on the side of his knee.

It is a generally accepted custom that when men appear on stage in tights they have jock straps on underneath. A young actor who broke this rule was accused by Noel Coward of having 'an entire Rockingham tea service' in his tights. And some years ago when the New York City Ballet were in Los Angeles, one of the male dancers appeared with tights but without jock strap. Whether this was for reasons of vanity or because he hadn't time to dress properly, history does not relate, but the fact that his tights tore in performance revealing all did make a small paragraph in the *Los Angeles Times*.

Somerset Maugham once invited Noel Coward, Beverly Nichols and Godfrey Winn to have lunch with him at his Mediterranean villa and meet the visiting American dramatist Edna St Vincent Millay. When he introduced them to her on the terrace overlooking the sea where they were to eat, she exclaimed to her host: 'Oh, Mr Maugham, but this is fairyland!'

Some homosexuals have a wicked way with women. Beverly Nichols would invite small groups of flower-loving ladies to visit his beautiful garden, and offer them tea afterwards. He would press several cups on them and then when they asked if they could slip out to 'spend a penny' would show them the way to the loo. There, the hapless ladies were confronted with a cruel dilemma, for inside the lavatory bowl Beverly had placed a vast and quite stunning arrangement of roses.

Gerald Crozier was a New York literary agent, a notorious homosexual and an incorrigible practical joker. He had a favourite trick that he liked to use whenever he was dining at a sufficiently grand and fashionable restaurant. Gerald would wait until a beautiful woman had come into the restaurant and been escorted to her table. He would then summon the wine waiter and ask him to deliver a note to the lady's table. He would tell the wine waiter not to say who the note had come from, but to wait for a reply. The wine waiter would then carry Gerald's note over to the lady, who would open it and read, 'I know I'm only the wine waiter here, but believe me I can uncork more than bottles! If you want the lay of your life, I'm your man. How about it, honey?'

'A thing of beauty is a boy forever' was one of Lytton Strachey's favourite maxims. During the First World War he was asked what he would do if he found his sister being raped by a German. Strachey replied that he would be man enough to interpose himself.

In 1978 a professor from Harvard University suffered something of a sexual humiliation when he offered to make a contribution to the world-famous Californian sperm bank. His offer was declined because the sperm banks won't accept deposits from known gays, be they Michelangelo, Leonardo da Vinci or Harvard professors.

Some homosexuals have a particular penchant for public lavatories. They go there in the hope of making new friends in congenial surroundings. It doesn't always work out that way. Since loitering in a gentlemen's convenience is against the law in most Western countries, the list of well-known names who have been caught with their trousers down in a public lavatory is a long one. Some of them, of course, are deliberately courting disaster: the risks add to the thrills. For others the threat of arrest is wholly unwelcome.

For Gerry Roberts of Eastbourne in Sussex it was a double disaster. His wife was a lavatory attendant and when she heard noises coming from inside one of the cubicles of the public lavatory that was her responsibility, she called the police. They came and broke down the lavatory door, revealing two very sheepish-looking middle-aged men: Mrs Roberts's husband Gerry and her younger brother George.

Laurie Simmonds was on his own in a public convenience in Torquay one afternoon hoping 'to pick up a bit of trade before tea'. Unfortunately for him no one seemed to be passing by. Laurie sat in hope in a cubicle and waited. After a while he dozed off and slept peacefully until roused by the noise of hammering. Emerging from his cloistered cubicle Laurie found that the local council had just boarded up the entrance to the lavatory and that he was now entombed. Eventually his cries for help were heard, the workmen released him, and the police arrested him for 'loitering with intent'.

Because his mother had wanted a daughter, the turn-of-the-century German poet Rainer Maria Rilke spent the first six years of his life dressed as a girl and addressed as Sophie.

By contrast the drama critic Alexander Woolcott's mother definitely wanted a son, but Alexander would have preferred to be a daughter. He wept openly at his inability to have children and was never happier than when going out to dinner dressed as a woman. Not for nothing is he famous for saying: 'All the things I really like to do are either illegal, immoral, or fattening.'

The Opening of the New York Assembly in 1702 was marked by the new English Governor's determination to appear on behalf of his cousin Queen Anne in more than name. His arrival in a blue silk evening gown, cut to the latest fashion, a diamond-studded headdress and satin shoes convinced most of those present that the American Revolution couldn't come any too quickly. Lord Cornbury was unabashed at their outrage. 'You are all very stupid people not to see the propriety of it all,' he told them in words that could have been chosen with greater diplomatic delicacy. 'In this place and on this occasion, I represent a woman, and in all respects I ought to represent her as faithfully as I can.' He was true to his word.

Although heavily built, with a round, fleshy face, Lord Cornbury contrived to make himself as presentable as the quirks of fashion would allow. He wore stays to give himself a figure and employed the leading dressmakers and milliners to augment his amply filled wardrobe. He habitually changed frocks to suit morning, afternoon and evening wear, once even leaving an official reception to slip into something more becoming. He took particular pleasure in promenading through New York or sitting fanning himself at an open window in full view of the bemused citizenry.

Cornbury served as Governor for seven years, a testament to his staying power and the tolerance of the New World. Eventually New York's dignitaries refused to deal any longer with petticoat government and Queen Anne was forced to recall her cousin. His sartorial extravagances had landed him deeply in debt to his dressmaker and he was packed off to prison until he was solvent again. Whether to a man's or woman's prison is not recorded.

In 1982 a Spanish waiter in London had something of a shock when he picked up a couple of girls in his car and began making advances to the one sitting beside him. The other 'girl' in the back seat then clobbered him with her handbag and turned out to be a six-foot Coldstream Guard in drag.

A London man whose girlfriend threatened to ditch him unless he learned what it was like to be a woman was arrested a few days later for impersonating a nun. The woman police officer who arrested him said that her suspicions were aroused when she realized this was the first time she had seen a nun wearing stiletto heels.

According to the *News of the World*, 'Pauline Jenkins had a "hell of a shock" on her wedding night when she discovered that her husband was a woman. "I threatened to leave there and then," she said. "But I went downstairs and made a cup of tea instead." '

A jury in Wayne County Circuit Court awarded $200,000 in damages to twenty-seven-year-old Carmon Leo following a road accident in which his car had been struck from the rear. Physically his injuries were restricted to his back but Leo's lawyer maintained that the accident had had far-reaching implications for his client's personality by turning him into a homosexual.

According to Leo his injuries had kept him away from work for six months, which brought its own problems. 'When I found I couldn't function in the business world and support my wife, the effect was emasculating,' he claimed. His lawyer told the court how Leo had returned to live with his parents after the accident and had begun to frequent homosexual bars and to read gay literature.

The jury awarded his wife $25,000 for the loss of a husband.

In a frank heart-to-heart with *The People* newspaper Lord Colin Campbell, brother to the Duke of Argyll, recounted his brief nine months of married bliss in America:

'I proposed to her across a candle-lit table in a restaurant at 3 o'clock in the morning and with twelve pints of draught Guinness under my belt. We spent our first night together as man and wife at a hotel in Philadelphia. She became the most passionate wife I could possibly hope that she might be, but alas, our fairy-tale marriage began to disintegrate when twenty-five-year-old Georgie, my wife, confessed that she had been a boy until the age of eighteen and had undergone a sex change. The only thing now is to pick up the pieces. I have to be married to a woman who can give me a family. This is a responsibility to the Argyll Clan.'

For Michael Clark a change of sex meant disaster because it also involved a change of occupation. As a man he had served with distinction in the United States Navy until 1969. When he became a woman, he was expected to leave the navy. This distressed him considerably and he was unhappy for several years until, in 1975, as Joanna Clark, he joined the US army, the only person ever known to have served in the American armed services as both a man and a woman.

In 1983 globe-trotting sales executive Keith Hull faced the ultimate sexual disaster: either change sex or die! Mr Hull, a happily married man with three children, returned from a business trip abroad with a rare tropical disease. Doctors told him he had no alternative but to have a sex-change operation or face death. Understandably Mr Hull chose to carry on living so he said goodbye to his wife, au revoir to his children and hello to 'Stephanie Anne Lloyd', his new persona. As Stephanie Lloyd the former Keith Hull went back to work as normal, and according to the *Daily Mirror* everybody took his change of sex in their stride. Thirty-seven-year-old Stephanie declared: 'I enjoyed life to the full as a man and I intend to do so as a woman.'

PUPPY LOVE

'Most parents don't worry about a
daughter until she fails to show up for
breakfast . . . then it's too late.'

Frank McKinney Hubbard

'It was some kind of shock. His nanny made a pass at
him when he was twelve years old.'

For many young people about to set out on the high road to sexual adventure the first problem is where to turn for sound advice...

The *Singapore Free Press* featured this heartfelt letter sent by a young man in love to the island's famous 'Uncle Joe' Problem Page:
  'I am an Indian, aged 19, and I'm in love with a 15-year-old Eurasian schoolgirl. I fell in love with her when she was 13, but I was forced to "break-off" with her recently. The reasons for this are (1) She does not seem to care for me of late; (2) She has started to mix with a set of bad girls; (3) She thinks she can boss everybody. Also I have a suspicion that she thinks I love someone else. Have I done right by breaking away from her? What shall I do?'

Uncle Joe answered:
  'I am getting rather "fed up" with people who keep on writing on both sides of the paper, as you have done. The next time anybody does this, I'm going to throw his letter into the waste-paper basket and say nothing.'

A few years ago a girl with a special personal problem wrote for advice to *Woman's Sphere*:
  'I am 15, and I often see a boy on the bus when I go home from work. I always try to sit by him because I like him very much but he won't have anything to do with me. I work in a fish and chip shop and never seem to get rid of the smell. Do you think this is the trouble?'

'Dear Marje,' began a letter sent to *Woman's Mirror*. 'If a girl has intercourse and then has nothing more to do with boys for a year, can she become a virgin again?'

It was signed 'Hopeful'.

There's nothing new in not knowing much about the facts of life. 'Erection,' wrote Aristotle in the third century BC, 'is chiefly caused by parsnips, artichokes, turnips, asparagus, candied ginger, acorns bruised to powder and drunk in muscadel, scallion, sea shellfish, etc . . .' The great philosopher was also of the opinion that a child's appearance could be determined by the mother: 'If in the act of copulation, the woman earnestly looks on the man, and fixes her mind on him, the child will resemble the father. Nay, if a woman, even in unlawful copulation, fix her mind upon her husband, the child will resemble him though he did not beget it.'

Nowadays sexual ignorance is less common because sex education is rife. In schools throughout the Western world they show sex education films – not as an end of term treat, but as part of the curriculum.

Sex education has come to be accepted as a Good Thing because when it comes to sex it seems that ignorance isn't bliss. As a middle-aged married woman put it at a teachers' conference recently: 'Sex education is so important. I didn't know what a homosexual was until I met my husband.'

Inevitably not everyone feels the same way. According to the *Ruislip-Northwood Gazette*, a speaker at another conference on the same subject had this to say:

'I contend that you cannot teach sex as a scientific subject, as it is treated in the school. Call it science and the children will want to experiment. I believe that there has been trouble with this already.'

And the British delegate at a teachers' convention in Baltimore, Maryland, was even more determined in his view. 'Why have sex education in our schools?' he asked. 'I was brought up before the era of sex education and I managed to get by. Don't forget, there is not a rabbit warren in the land where they show sex education films and yet this has never been a problem for the rabbits of the world. Indeed, those of you who are of a literary bent will recall that Peter Rabbit was not an only child. There was Flopsy and Mopsy and Cottontail as well as Peter. And doubtless there would have been many more had it not been for that unfortunate accident which befell Mr Rabbit in Mr MacGregor's garden whereby he ended up in one of Mrs MacGregor's rabbit pies. Doubtless Beatrix Potter felt it was a neater finish to the story than a vasectomy.'

Young people are occasionally confronted with the facts of life at a very tender age.

Richard Olivier, the son of Sir Laurence Olivier and Joan Plowright, was only a little boy when, on the front at Brighton, he was confronted by the sight of two dogs mating. The lad turned to Noel Coward, who was the Oliviers' house guest, and said, 'What are they doing, Uncle Noel?'

'The one in front is blind,' said Coward unperturbed, 'and the one behind is being very, very sweet and pushing him all the way to St Dunstan's.'

That sex education may be necessary is clear judging from some of the replies given by a group of five- to seven-year-olds from New York State who were asked 'How are babies made?' Their answers included several gems:

– 'Mom makes babies with Dr Roberts. I dunno how they do it.'

- 'If a man and woman love each other very, very much the woman will grow a baby inside her body.'
- 'Dad has a carrot that he plants in Mom's cabbage patch. About a year later the baby has been grown.'
- 'Mom collects the babies from the hospital where they are born somehow.'
- 'Mom takes a pill every day and it's a baby pill. It makes a baby grow inside her tummy. When it's one year old it comes out of her and cries.'
- 'Mom and Dad are happy together and then a baby comes along.'
- 'The father gives the mother plenty of money. If he gives her enough, she goes out and gets a baby.'
- 'To have a baby you go on a special diet and eat spinach and coal and stuff. Then you get real fat and that's the baby inside you. When you are so fat, the doctor cuts you open and gets the baby.'
- 'Dad and Mom fuck.'

Teaching children about sex has its risks. At the Park School, Baltimore, Maryland, a pupil tampered with the box of transparencies prior to the sex education slide-show so that during the lesson, when tasteful drawings of the human anatomy were supposed to appear on the screen, raunchy *Playboy*-style nude studies appeared instead.

Disaster can strike when sex education teachers get too involved in their subject.

Two girls at a Sixth Form College in Cambridge were

discussing the new biology master. 'Doesn't he dress well?' said one of them. 'And so quickly too,' said the other.

The story is apocryphal, of course, but the case of Vera Rainbird, a biology teacher from Sunderland, is true. Miss Rainbird taught at a boys' grammar school until the headmaster came into her classroom one day and found her sitting on her desk with a naked sixteen-year-old on either side of her.

The headmaster gave Miss Rainbird the sack, but she took him and the local education authority to an industrial tribunal claiming wrongful dismissal. Miss Rainbird said she was teaching human biology and that the naked boys were helping her give a demonstration to the rest of the class. She lost her case.

Some are younger than others when they have their first taste of sex. A seventeen-year-old girl was recently seen in the King's Road, Chelsea, sporting a tee-shirt with the message 'I AM A VIRGIN' printed on the front. On the back it said, 'THIS IS A VERY OLD TEE-SHIRT'.

According to the definitive work on the subject, *The First Time* by Karl Fleming and Anne Taylor Fleming, Debbie Reynolds remained a virgin until she married Eddie Fisher at the age of twenty-three, while David Niven was introduced to the delights of sex by a Soho prostitute called Nessie when he was a mere lad of fourteen. Victoria Principal was almost eighteen when she started (in the front seat of a car), Dyan Cannon was seventeen (and on the rug at home with a choirboy), Art Buchwald was fifteen (and seduced by a hotel chambermaid), while Mae West was just thirteen when her music teacher took advantage of her for the first time. Appropriately for the lady who made 'Come up and see me sometime' her catchphrase, it happened half-way up the stairs.

Once young people have been introduced to sex anything can happen and the pace can be alarming. This report of one maiden's fall comes from the *Daily Mail*:

'She was picked up by two men as she got off the bus at Victoria coach station. Within minutes she was drinking coffee with them. Within hours she was no longer a virgin. Within a week she was being sold to rich Americans and Arabs in a four-star hotel. She realised too late what was happening to her.'

Early in 1978 the Swedish Supreme Court ruled in favour of a ninety-two-year-old farm worker who had taken out a paternity suit against a seventy-five-year-old postman. In the course of her submission, the farm-worker told the court: 'I was hoeing a turnip field in Southern Skare in 1924 when a cyclist arrived, dismounted and became the father of my child.'

When asked how she could recognize the postman after fifty-four years, she replied confidently, 'Because of his exceptional ugliness.'

In 1980 young Linda Boller of Des Moines, Iowa and her teenage fiancé Max were only a fortnight away from their wedding day when Linda's parents went out for the evening and asked her to babysit for her younger brother. Left alone together after the little boy had gone to bed, Linda and Max cuddled on the sofa. They were rapidly ready for more adventurous fun and games and decided to go upstairs to Linda's bedroom.

It was when they were both naked in bed that Linda remembered the washing her mother had asked her to take out of the machine. Worried that leaving it inside might suggest that she had been up to no good, Linda, still starkers, ran downstairs, with Max chasing after her offering to help. As they made their way through the dark a voice called out, 'Guess who?' – and the lights suddenly went full on!

Linda's parents had arranged a surprise pre-wedding party for friends, neighbours and relatives, with the priest who was to marry them as guest of honour.

A Yugoslav man who organized an elopement with his neighbour's young daughter spirited away the maiden in a blanket one night and in his excitement drove for ten minutes before daring to stop the car and greet his love. Gently lifting the blanket from her face he found himself looking deep into the eyes of her seventy-three-year-old grandmother, who took advantage of his state of shock and beat him up.

The trouble with sex is that it can lead to pregnancy, particularly when young people are given advice on contraception that is either misleading or misunderstood. Back in 1868 Dr Russell Thacker Trall's *Sexual Physiology* became a bestseller and was widely read by university undergraduates because in his magisterial work Dr Trall claimed that during journeys to the Friendly Isles and Iceland he had come across 'some women (who) have that flexibility and vigour of the whole muscular system that they can, by effort of will, prevent conception'. Dr Trall's eager young readers also learnt that 'sometimes coughing or sneezing will have the same effect. Running, jumping, lifting and dancing are often resorted to successfully.'

Modern contraceptive methods can also create difficulties. In 1974 a London GP wrote to the *Evening Standard* to report the case of a teenage girl for whom he had prescribed the Pill. According to the doctor, who assured readers this was no joke, the girl came back a month later asking for a different form of contraception. 'What's wrong with the Pill?' asked the GP. 'It keeps falling out,' answered the girl.

Recently in St Albans in Hertfordshire, a seventeen-year-old boy went to have dinner with his new girlfriend and her parents. It was a much more formal dinner than the young man had expected, but he sensed he was carrying it off with a certain debonair style until, towards the end of the first course, he felt the urge to sneeze. Pulling his handkerchief out of his breast pocket he brought a contraceptive sheath out with the hankie. The contraceptive fell into his bowl of soup. Not knowing what to do to cover his embarrassment or how to get rid of the offending item, he scooped it into his soup spoon and popped it into his mouth. Try as he might he couldn't swallow it. The contraceptive remained in his mouth until the end of the meal when he asked to be excused and rushed to the lavatory. There he threw it into the loo and flushed it furiously. To his dismay, the contraceptive wouldn't sink. Becoming increasingly distraught he waited in the loo and flushed the lavatory six times more. Each time the buoyant contraceptive remained obstinately afloat. When he had been in the loo for fifteen minutes, he decided to abandon hope and his girlfriend. He emerged from the loo, announced to his hosts that he felt extremely unwell and made a hasty retreat.

A sixteen-year-old Vancouver girl who had been having sex with her boyfriend for several months started to worry that he might get fed up with having to take the contraceptive precautions himself. She desperately wanted to take the Pill, but as her doctor was a close friend of her parents, she couldn't face asking him to help her.

Then one day she found her mother's pills while helping with the housework and, not having a firm grasp of the principles of contraception, substituted some of these with aspirins.

The girl and her boyfriend were delighted with the new arrangement until a few months later when the *mother* announced that *she* was pregnant.

Discovering what your children are up to can be a disconcerting experience for a parent. A correspondent wrote to *Woman* magazine in considerable distress:

'Nosey-parkering isn't my weakness, but I recently found in my son's jacket evidence that he must consort with women. It was a terrible blow. It's worse because I can't talk of it to anyone – neither his father nor himself. I wouldn't mind so much if he was engaged; it would be wrong but understandable. This is just vice.'

After being summoned to appear before the Woking Bench in answer to an affiliation order a local man replied in writing: 'I don't know whether or not I am the father of the child. I am only an apprentice.'

The innocence of young people can be very refreshing. A teenage couple from Conway in Ireland were plighting their troth at the altar when the bride complained of feeling unwell and asked to be helped to a pew. There she gave birth to a bouncing baby boy.

'It was the first I had heard of it,' announced the groom. 'But Dora is an assistant nurse so she knew exactly what to do. When it was over we carried on with the wedding as if nothing had happened.'

If people can have babies in unlikely places, they can conceive them in unusual settings too.

Embarrassed prison officials in Italy recently found themselves landed with the tricky job of explaining a major breach in security when it was announced that one of the prisoners held in a maximum security wing was expecting a baby. The youthful mother-to-be flatly refused to identify the father and with the Minister for Justice demanding a full-scale enquiry one harassed official told reporters: 'This sort of thing makes nonsense of our claims that Italy's maximum security prisons are impregnable.'

For some newly-weds the problem isn't having children, it's *not* having them.

After determined efforts to conceive a child, a young Yugoslav husband working in Germany went with his wife to a family planning clinic where they were told that the husband was sterile. Fortunately the young couple were on excellent terms with their German neighbours, who had two children of their own. The German husband was prevailed upon to help the Yugoslav and his wife. For a fee of around £1,500 the German agreed to sleep with the Yugoslav bride for three nights a week until she became pregnant.

Sadly, after six months he had been no more successful than her husband, so the German decided that he too should visit the family planning clinic. He did and was told that he also was sterile. Then the trouble really started. His own wife was forced to come clean and confess that her children had been fathered by another man. And to add injury to insult the Yugoslav sued him for breach of contract.

Some people desperately want to have babies. Others most definitely don't. In April 1974 Mr Frank Speck of Philadelphia had a vasectomy. Several months later his wife became pregnant. She opted for an abortion which was performed in December by another doctor. A short time after that she gave birth to a daughter. The Specks sued both doctors.

SPIRITUAL REFRESHMENT

'Platonic friendship: the interval
between the introduction and the first
kiss.'

Sophie Irene Loeb

'I found your confession most interesting. Would
you like me to ghost your autobiography?'

Sex and religion have long been closely associated, often with disastrous consequences. At the start of the First Crusade in 1191 Richard the Lionheart landed at Marseilles and discovered to his dismay that his advance party had squandered all the campaign funds on prostitutes.

In 1714 the Roman Catholic Church did away with the requirement that men confessing fornication must name their partners. Evidence had come to light that too many priests had been making improper use of the information.

Clergymen, of all denominations, have always taken a lively interest in sex...

The Very Reverend Martin Sullivan, the late Dean of St Paul's Cathedral in London, used to tell the story of the randy Bishop from New Zealand who, when he retired, returned to the old family farmstead and decided to use his savings to build a swimming pool in a field behind the farmhouse. Showing the architect who was to design the pool where he wanted it positioned, the Bishop said to him, 'Please be sure you don't disturb that tree there, because it was directly under that tree that I first had sex.'

The architect was slightly abashed to find a Bishop, albeit a retired Bishop, confiding in him in this way, but promised that the tree would be unharmed.

'Yes,' said the Bishop, 'it takes me back a few years, as you can imagine.'

'Yes, I can,' said the architect quietly.

'And that tree over there,' continued the Bishop, 'I don't want you disturbing that one either. That's where her mother stood watching us.'

This was too much for the architect. 'I don't believe it, Bishop! Her mother stood watching while you had sex with her daughter?'

'That's right,' said the Bishop.

'But what did the mother say?'

'Baaa.'

The French have never had much respect for their clergy, suspecting they pursue their careers without letting their calling interfere with their enjoyment of life's baser pleasures. So when an eminent cleric was unexpectedly called to meet his celestial boss while actually 'on the job' in a Parisian brothel, there was understandable consternation at the potential for ridicule if the fact ever got out.

Fortunately the brothel's enterprising Madame managed to get the deceased clergyman's still-warm corpse back into its robes and dragged it downstairs to the foyer. She then telephoned his office and a story was hurriedly concocted that the good man had merely taken shelter in the doorway of the building during a sudden and severe storm. Unfortunately the press proved irritatingly sceptical of this explanation and an enterprising journalist, posing as a customer, penetrated the depths of the establishment to discover more.

Seeing one of the girls who seemed still visibly shaken by an upsetting experience he offered her a sympathetic shoulder on which to unburden herself. Relieved to be able to get the whole thing off her chest and confide in a friendly stranger she poured out the entire story, summing up her ordeal with the poignant cry, *'Ah, Monsieur, je croyais qu'il venait! Mais il allait!'* ('I thought he was coming! But he was going!')

A former Bishop of Lincoln happened to drop in on one of his vicars at the start of a confirmation class and accepted the invitation to stay and listen to the candidates that were soon to be presented to him. The vicar asked one of the girls to define the state of matrimony. 'It's a state of terrible torment which those who enter are compelled to undergo for a time to prepare them for a better world,' she replied nervously.

'No, no, my dear,' said the vicar. 'That's not matrimony. That's the definition of purgatory.'

'Never mind,' said the bishop, 'perhaps the child has been shown the light.'

Annoyed that no one answered when he called at a house that he had gone out of his way to visit, the Rev. Leonard Waley of Longford, Derbyshire, left a terse note: 'Revelations 3:20: "Behold I stand at the door and knock: if anyone hears my voice and opens the door I will come to him."'

As the congregation was leaving church the following Sunday one of the parish ladies handed him a card bearing the inscription: 'Genesis 3:10: "I heard the sound of thee in the garden and I was afraid, because I was naked and hid myself."'

There was a minor disaster in the Vatican a few years ago when a newsreader broadcasting in French on the Vatican Radio Station, instead of saying *'la population immense du Cape'*, referred to *'la copulation immense du Pape'*.

In 1979 in Chesterfield a vicar whose thoughts had long since risen above the earthly level of those of his flock was heard telling the congregation at a wedding: 'Sometimes in a marriage the couple have been known to get on top of each other...'

In the same year in Badgastein, Austria, disaster struck a more worldly clergyman who was caught with his cassock up and his trousers down in the confessional. He was supposed to be hearing the confession of a young bride whose wedding he was to conduct a month later. In fact, he was introducing her to the delights of oral sex.

No one would have known about any of this had the priest and the bride-to-be not been unexpectedly disturbed by a young policeman who had called in at the church hoping to have his own confession heard. Disturbed by the less than ecclesiastical murmurings emanating from the confessional, the policeman pulled back the curtain to reveal the priest with the young lady – who unhappily turned out to be his own twenty-two-year-old fiancée.

Father Brian O'Donovan of Cork tells what he professes to be the true story of the young Irish girl who went to confession full of apprehension and too embarrassed to put into words what was troubling her conscience.

'Oh, Father, I don't know how to tell you, sure,' she stammered.

'Come, come, my daughter,' replied the priest, 'let me help you. Now, was it a sin of the flesh?'

'It was, Father,' said the girl.

'And was it with a man?' asked the priest.

'It was, Father.'

'And tell me, daughter, was it against your will?'

'Oh no, Father, it was against the kitchen dresser. And sure it would have done yer heart good to hear the cups a-rattlin'.'

'Hearing nuns' confessions,' said Monsignor Ronald Knox, 'is like being nibbled to death by geese.'

In fact, nuns occasionally do have something of substance to confess. For example, a few years ago there was the case of the young nun who went to her Reverend Mother to confess that she was pregnant.

'Go to the kitchen,' said the Reverend Mother severely, 'and drink a cup of vinegar and the juice of six lemons.'

'But that won't get rid of the baby,' the young nun protested.

'Perhaps not,' said the Reverend Mother, 'but at least it will wipe that smug grin off your face.'

The story is apocryphal, of course, but to prove that truth can be stranger than fiction, in 1968 the *New York Times* reported the case of a nun from São Paulo in Brazil who over a period of six years had three children by two different fathers. Her Mother Superior only got to hear about it when the nun became pregnant for the fourth time and decided, apparently reluctantly, to abandon her vocation.

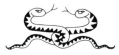

In his autobiography, *Foreign Correspondent*, the American reporter Dan Andersen told the story – again, one hopes, apocryphal – of how he had interviewed the Mother Superior of a convent just outside Pisa in the spring of 1947. He asked her about the horrors of war.

'The fascists were beasts,' she told him. 'They broke into the convent here and raped every nun, except Sister Angelina. The Germans were horrible. They came and raped every nun, except Sister Angelina. And I am sorry to tell you, the Americans were no better. They came too and they raped every nun – except Sister Angelina.'

'What's wrong with Sister Angelina?' asked Andersen.

'Ah,' replied the Mother Superior serenely. 'She's not keen on that kind of thing.'

Saint Matthew's warning, 'Beware of false prophets', may have come as some relief to readers of the *Church Militant* who one day opened its pages to discover this dire prediction: 'In the future, when man learns to control his disordered impulses ... the time will come when the sex organs will atrophy and disappear and man will produce his kind from his larynx, which will be transformed to speak the Creative Word ... Meanwhile, we must make the best of a bad job.'

Readers of a Catholic parish magazine in San Bernadino, California, were let in for an even greater surprise when they opened the Christmas issue in December 1969. To liven up the pages of the depressingly conservative magazine the new priest had decided to feature a selection of what he described as 'witty limericks about men and women of the cloth'.

The good people of San Bernadino were quite broadminded. They even managed wan smiles as they read the first two or three verses in the priest's collection:

> The Dean undressed
> With heaving breast
> The bishop's wife to lie on.
> He thought it lewd
> To do it nude
> So he kept his old school tie on.

> There was a young monk of Kilkyre
> Was smitten with carnal desire
> The immediate cause
> Was the abbess's drawers
> Which were hung up to dry by the fire.

There was a young monk from Siberia
Whose morals were very inferior.
  He did to a nun
  What he shouldn't have done
And now she's a Mother Superior.

But others in the collection were clearly less acceptable:

There once was a priest of Gibraltar
Who wrote dirty jokes in his psalter.
  An inhibited nun
  Who had read every one
Made a vow to be laid on his altar.

There was a young man of St Giles
Who'd walked thousands and thousands of miles
  From the Cape of Good Hope
  Just to bugger the Pope
But he couldn't – the pontiff had piles.

There was a young Bishop from Brest
Who openly practised incest.
  'My sisters and nieces
  Are all fancy pieces
And they don't cost a cent,' he confessed.

There was a young rector of Kings
Whose mind was on heavenly things
  But his heart was on fire
  For a boy in the choir
Whose ass was like jelly on springs.

Understandably the parishioners of San Bernadino felt they had no alternative but to report their priest to his Bishop. Equally understandably, the Bishop asked for the priest's resignation. The young man gave it with a good grace and decided to give up the priesthood. A year later he published a collection of licentious limericks and dedicated the book to his Bishop.

Not all clergymen are equally broad-minded. Some years ago, a Yorkshire vicar who had spent his declining years looking with disdain at his daughter's immodest dress left her a considerable fortune in his will, but with one string attached:

'Seeing that my daughter Anna has not availed herself of my advice touching the objectionable practice of going about with her arms bare to the elbows, my will is that, should she continue after my death this violation of the modesty of her sex, all the goods, chattels, moneys, land, and other that I have devised to her for the maintenance of her future life shall pass to the oldest of the sons of my sister Caroline.

'Should anyone take exception to this my wish as being too severe, I answer that licence in dress in a woman is a mark of a depraved mind.'

While some clergymen can be alarmingly censorious, by no means all of them are. A priest in Columbus, Ohio, encouraged newly-wed couples to have their first taste of married sex in his church and on the altar if they wished. He liked to watch, but, he insisted, 'only if invited'. Unfortunately when the bishop got to hear about the post-marital goings-on in Columbus he didn't approve and firmly asked the priest for his resignation. The priest had no alternative but to go, though he told reporters he couldn't understand why he had been dismissed. 'Married sex is a sacrament, after all,' he said. 'What more beautiful gift could a young couple offer to God?'

What is and is not considered acceptable depends on who is doing the considering. As they say, it's all in the eye of the

beholder. Believe it or not, Michelangelo's efforts on the
ceiling of the Sistine Chapel by no means met with universal
approval from his contemporaries. Pope Paul IV was
horrified by them and ordered their removal on the grounds
of obscenity. Fortunately for posterity there was an outcry
against this. A compromise was struck and Michelangelo's
pupil, Danielle de Voltera, was engaged to 'dress' all the
figures in *The Last Judgement*, including all the angels and the
Virgin Mary, whom his master had thoughtlessly left as
naked as God had made them.

More recently, in London, the unveiling of the statue of
Achilles representing the invincibility of the Duke of Wel-
lington sent shock waves through the crowd gathered in
Hyde Park when it became clear they were witnessing the
unveiling of the nation's first nude statue. The embarrassment was all the greater as the statue had been provided by
the women of England in gratitude for his services. Modesty was restored within a short time when Achilles
sprouted a tactful fig leaf.

Even Britain's outstanding archaeological features are not
safe from the easily-offended. 'Now that a campaign has
courageously been started against "shop nudes", may I
draw attention to the Wilmington Giant,' pleaded a correspondent to the *Eastbourne Herald Chronicle*.

'For many years I have wished to ask my aunt to visit our
beautiful town but have been deterred from doing so by the
knowledge that she would have to pass this stark, staring
figure.

'Surely it would be possible to fit this disgusting effigy

with some kind of Hessian kilt; or, failing this, perhaps a strategically planted row of shrubbery might serve.'

Yet while one section of the population is taking umbrage at too much attention to detail, another section is deploring a lack of authenticity.

Following the publication of a letter in the *Guardian* about the shortcomings of doll manufacturers, another reader wrote to the paper: 'As a mother of three daughters and a pre-school playground superintendent, I should like to say how much I agree with Mrs Van Tweest (Letters, October 9) about the way in which our fear-and-guilt-ridden toy manufacturers shy away from producing male dolls complete with genitalia. My 8-year-old daughter has been indignant on this subject for several years now – and from a very early age used modelling clay to remedy deficiencies.'

The unveiling of a plaque at City Hall, Prince George, British Columbia, promised to be about as exciting as every other such unveiling, so Peter Duffy, a photographer, sent to cover the event, chose to add a little excitement to the proceedings by sticking a large pin-up nude over the plaque.

'The mayor didn't see the picture at first,' he explained after the event, 'but when he did his mouth just hung open. Instead of the usual ripple of applause, there was absolute silence. Then I was sacked.'

1959 was an important landmark in the moral welfare of America. That was the year in which SINA – the Society for Indecency to Naked Animals (*sic*) – came into being.

The first the nation heard of its crusade to stem the exposure of the sexual organs of pets, livestock and zoo animals was on the *Today* show on TV which included an interview with G. Clifford Trout, the president of the Society. This earnest young man had inherited $400,000 from his late father for the sole purpose of promoting the Society's aims. As Trout told his interviewer: 'Don't let your moral standards go lower and lower due to naked animals. It's a shocking situation, and I am spending every single minute of every day and every last dollar of my father's money to correct this evil.'

Word started to get around about SINA. Leaflets appeared claiming a membership of 55,000. Visitors to the Society's New York headquarters found the walls hung with pictures of dogs, cats, pigs, sheep, cattle and many other animals all decently clad in morally approved clothing. *Life* magazine organized a photographic session featuring a collection of dogs belonging to Society members all sporting natty briefs.

After its initial burst of publicity SINA slipped from the pinnacle of public notice and was left to get on with its work. When an airline placed a 'naked' papier maché horse in the window of its Manhattan office, SINA complained to the Fifth Avenue Association and the horse was quickly removed; SINA also received an apology. On the West Coast the *San Francisco Chronicle* ran a two-part article on SINA which featured Mr Trout trying to help a fawn at the city's zoo into a pair of underpants. This sparked off renewed public interest, with editorials across the continent citing SINA as evidence of the nation's growing hysteria. The final accolade came when, three years after his first appearance on *Today*, Trout was invited to appear on Walter Cronkite's evening show on CBS to discuss SINA and its future plans. At this point SINA's future was suddenly cut short. One of the CBS staff noticed Trout's extraordinary resemblance to actor Buck Henry, who had recently joined the network as a writer for one of its other shows. Further investigations revealed that they were one and the same man.

With his cover blown Henry made a clean breast of the SINA affair and admitted to having been recruited by hoaxer Alan Abel to appear as G. Clifford Trout. SINA had been a gigantic and absurdly successful spoof from start to finish, inspired by Abel's amusement at the mixed reactions of a group of people who had witnessed a bull mounting a cow in the middle of a road in Texas.

Prudery can take many forms. In 1973 cars in New York began to display new golden licence plates with three numbers and three letters in blue. The Department of Motor Vehicles was proud that the new plates, designed to replace the old blue plates with yellow numbers, 'offer an almost infinite number of combinations', but was nervous about where some of those combinations might lead. The department was 'determined to avoid sequences of letters that are obscene, suggestive or insulting', and so put a ban on WET and DRY, on PIG and RAT, on FAG and DYK, on FEM and GYP, on ODD and POT, as well, of course, as the more obvious SEX and SIN.

When Dr Kinsey published his report on the sexual behaviour of the human male in 1948 it attracted the predictable cries of outrage from offended guardians of public morality, one of the most spirited of which stated that the entire project was a fruitless waste of time, confirming as it did the writer's conviction that 'the male population is a herd of prancing, leering goats'.

How true. As Mae West was fond of observing, 'Give a man a free hand and he'll run it all over you.'

Some time ago the US Supreme Court elected to return the power of censoring pornography to local authorities and in accordance with this the town of Clarkstown, New York, set up a nine-member 'obscenity committee'. Harry Snyder, a retired businessman, was chosen as chairman, an interesting appointment in view of his blindness.

Interviewed after the appointment a delighted Mr Snyder admitted that the committee had attracted a good deal of local interest. 'My phone hasn't stopped ringing since.' When he was asked how he was able to carry out his new role, the chairman explained that other members of the committee sat next to him during film shows 'to fill me in when the screen goes silent'.

Of course, it is not only prudes and priests who take a professional interest in sex. It is very much part of the prostitute's life as well. And not surprisingly members of 'the oldest profession' and their clients turn out to be as disaster-prone as everyone else.

Witness the case of Ms Lindi St Claire. At the end of 1980, with business booming, Lindi, a leading London 'disciplinarian' who specialized in providing stern 'correction' for her male clients, thought the time had come to register her activities as a business. The Registrar of Companies took a less open-minded view of her trade and refused to list her as a prostitute or even 'French-lesson teacher', offering instead to describe her work as providing 'personal services'. Ms St Claire took exception to this mealy-mouthed equivocation, and took the Registrar to court – but lost.

Her case attracted wide public interest, so wide that three days after St Valentine's Day, 1981 Inspectors from the Inland Revenue called to look over her premises, examine the capital assets that equipped her dungeon and prepare a tax assessment, which amounted to little short of £11,000.

Earlier in 1980, and again in London, neighbours in Ambleside Avenue, Streatham, were surprised to see police swarming out of squad cars and disappearing into number 32.

Inside the house the police found fifty-three men. Seventeen were standing in line on the stairs, each holding a luncheon voucher, and the rest were disported about the building enjoying the favours of a number of women. The clientele revealed that it was a brothel of some distinction. Apparently businessmen, barristers, accountants, a vicar, an MP and a member of the House of Lords were all to be found there. Each one had bought his luncheon voucher for £25 as a sex-ticket.

According to police reports 249 men and 50 women had arrived at the house in the preceding twelve days, though neighbours seemed surprised to find that Mrs Cynthia Payne, the householder, led anything other than a normal domestic life. The judge, however, was convinced that her life was far from normal, particularly as she had already appeared in court on four similar charges and on this occasion pleaded guilty to controlling three prostitutes. He fined her £2,000 and sentenced her to eighteen months imprisonment, later reduced to six.

The *China Post* reported the case of a Taiwanese couple who rowed so violently that the wife left home and had to be followed by her husband to the city of Kaohsiung. His search was fruitless and to console himself he went to a hotel for the night and asked for a call girl to cheer him up. The girl that knocked shyly at his door turned out to be his wife. The couple had another blazing row in the hotel but went home together afterwards 'for fear of losing face'.

After what can only be described as a nervous start to married life an Exeter man confided his problems to the *Southern Evening Echo*, telling one of the reporters:

'I admit I married my wife because she was a weight-lifter and after we had enjoyed ourselves she said she would beat me up unless I became her husband, but I received a profound shock when I discovered that she was also a prostitute.

'Two days after we were married I came home after drawing my social security and found the house full of Hell's Angels.

'My wife told me to wait in the kitchen until she had finished work. After a few minutes she came into the kitchen in tears. She said that one of the Hell's Angels had left the house in disgust as soon as she had taken her clothes off. When I tried to cheer her up she turned nasty and insisted that I became a prostitute too.

'It took me a few weeks to get into the job. But the charge that I am living off my wife's immoral earnings is quite untrue. We pool what we earn. It comes to about £9 a week, plus the security, and this is not enough to satisfy her longing for expensive clothes.

'We are both very unhappy, but we have decided to make a go of it.'

In 1978 in South Carolina, following a police raid on one of the state's most notorious brothels in which 800 clients were arrested, police headquarters were inundated with phone calls from desperate men frantically trying to have their names removed from the charge sheet. Among the hundreds of calls received was one from a seventy-three-year-old retired dentist who offered the police $100 to have his name added to the list of accused.

SWEET NOTHINGS

'Owing to the fuel crisis officials are advised to take advantage of their secretaries between the hours of 12 and 2.'

Office Notice.

'Dammit, how many guys do you need to make a quorum?'

Following a certain amount of misunderstanding over a social gathering in Maidstone, one of the organizers, a Mr Curry, explained the cause of the trouble: 'They were planning to call the get-together a cheese and wine party until I pointed out to them that it was illegal. We didn't want to get into trouble so we changed the name. We thought if we called it "cheese and you know what" everyone would think of wine. It's rather unfortunate.'

Some people have a special way with words. A forty-eight-year-old Southend woman, arrested in the town for prostitution, told magistrates that as she was blind in one eye and plagued with blurred vision in the other, she was hardly up to plying for trade in the streets, adding felicitously, 'I can only see if someone is right on top of me.'

Even when people mean what they say, they don't always say what they mean. The requests and applications made by members of the public to the US Department of Welfare in recent years have included some choice turns of phrase:

'My husband got his project cut off two weeks ago, and I haven't had any relief since.'

'Since I made an arrangement with the man in your office I am having a baby and my doctor says I should be getting even more of it.'

'I cannot get sick pay. I have six children. Can you tell me why?'

'Please send me a form for having babies at reduced prices.'

'I have heard there are more than two ways you can have it and it works out cheaper the more you get if you have it the other way.'

'This is my eighth child. What are you going to do about it?'

'Unless my husband gets money pretty soon I will be forced to lead an immortal life.'

The novelist and playwright Clemence Dane had a special gift for making the most innocent remark sound utterly outrageous. To her dinner guests she announced one evening: 'We're having roast cock tonight.' ... Arguing loudly with the actress Joyce Carey in the crowded foyer of the Old Vic theatre in London she exclaimed: 'But, Joyce, it's well known that Shakespeare sucked Bacon dry.' ...

When a friend asked about her goldfish, last seen in a pool catching the full rays of the blazing sun, she replied: 'Oh, they're all right now! They've got a vast erection covered with everlasting pea.' ... In one of her ghost stories she included the memorable line: 'Night after night for weeks she tried to make him come...'

It was when she decided to teach Noel Coward to sculpt that Miss Dane really came into her own: 'Noel, dear boy, you must wipe your tool! You cannot work with a dirty tool,' she told him briskly. Then she showed him how to work the clay on the armature: 'Now then, stick it right up, ram it, ram it, ram it and work away, either from the back or the front, whichever comes easiest! Some people use a lubricant, I've used honey in my time! And remember, when you've finished you must withdraw it wig-gle wag-gle, wig-gle, wig-gle, very gently.'

Clemence Dane, of course, was a complete innocent. Would that there were more like her!

A woman from Duxford, near Cambridge, who had

bought an ice-cream gateau for her tea, was appalled to find the word 'Sex' written across it in large white letters when she opened it at home.

The woman complained vigorously to the manufacturers who apologized profusely, sent her a replacement gateau and explained that the unexpected message had been put there maliciously by a worker who had just been given the sack.

A few years ago in Sunderland a little girl looking through her Granny's cards at Christmas was puzzled by the jingle on one of them. The grandmother asked her to read it aloud and the child began:

> A robin redbreast on my sill
> Sang for a crust of bread
> I slowly brought the window down
> And smashed its fucking head.

A spokesman for the Greeting Card Association who answered the grandmother's enquiry as to whether this was really the sort of message that embodied the spirit of Christmas, replied: 'This verse is about 120 years old and is well-known to card collectors.'

Some poetry is deliberately offensive. Most, of course, is not.

> The organ 'gins to swell;
> She's coming, she's coming!
> My lady comes at last.

So wrote William Makepeace Thackeray in his delightful – and wholly innocent – poem *At the Church Gate*.

If you are looking for filth you can always find it. You

might think you were safe enough reading Charlotte Brontë or Jane Austen or George Eliot, but if you have a mind to it – and an eye for it – you can unearth the most unfortunate lines in the most unlikely places:

He flourished his tool ... A warm excited thrill ran through my veins, my blood seemed to give a bound, and then raced fast and hot along its channels. I got up nimbly, came round to where he stood, and faced him.

From *The Professor* by Charlotte Brontë

... In winter his private balls were numerous enough for any young lady who was not suffering under the insatiable appetite for fifteen.

From *Sense and Sensibility* by Jane Austen

Mrs Glagg had doubtless the glossiest and crispest brown curls in her drawers, as well as curls in various degrees of fuzzy laxness.

From *Mill on the Floss* by George Eliot

Clearly some folk are incurably filthy-minded. However desirable, it seems it's just not possible to force people to *think clean*. It has been tried. At Kansas State University, for example, there is a legal stricture on the use of obscenity by faculty members on university property. Despite the rule, rumour has it that the teachers at Kansas State are as filthy-minded as those you would meet on any other college campus.

Of course, the happy corollary of not being able to force people to think clean is that you can't force them to think dirty either. And if you want evidence of that, here is what the American sporting magazine *Field and Stream* had to say when D. H. Lawrence's notorious novel *Lady Chatterley's Lover* made its first unexpurgated appearance in the United States in 1959:

Although written many years ago, *Lady Chatterley's Lover* has just been reissued by Grove Press, and this fictional account of the day-by-day life of an English gamekeeper is still of considerable interest to outdoor-minded readers, as it contains many passages on pheasant raising, the apprehending of poachers, ways to control vermin, and other chores and duties of the professional gamekeeper.

Unfortunately, one is obliged to wade through many pages of extraneous material in order to discover and savour these sidelights on the management of a Midland shooting estate, and in this reviewer's opinion the book cannot take the place of J. R. Miller's *Practical Gamekeeper*.

Innocence is always endearing. In 1984 the Schools Broadcasting unit of the BBC celebrated its Diamond Jubilee by repeating one of its most celebrated broadcasts. The programme was a music and movement class in which the lady teacher urged her young listeners to have fun with their balls:

'We are going to play a hiding and finding game. Now, are your balls high up or low down? Close your eyes a minute and dance around, and look for them. Are they high up? Or are they low down? If you have found your balls, toss them over your shoulder and play with them.'

When making a live radio or television broadcast it is all too easy to utter the apparently unutterable:

... Interviewing a recently appointed woman assistant governor at a man's prison Jack de Manio once asked: 'Do you think the prisoners will regard you as a good screw?'

... Peter West was talking about the seeding of players in the Wimbledon championships and innocently remarked:

'Jimmy Connors' wife is expecting a baby and there was some doubt about his entry.'

... At the 1976 Montreal Olympics a television commentator rose to the occasion splendidly as an exciting race reached its climax. 'And now,' he said, 'Juantorena opens wide his legs and shows his class.'

... Dan Maskell, covering a match in the Braniff Airways Men's Doubles tournament, allowed the patriotic efforts of David Lloyd and Mark Cox to get the better of him: 'The British boys are now adopting the attacking position – Cox up.'

The doyen of British cricket commentators and the undisputed master of the broadcast *faux pas* is Brian Johnston.

In the course of one match in Australia he described the field of play to the listening millions and then asked them to picture 'Neil Harvey standing with his legs apart waiting for a tickle.'

On a later occasion he welcomed listeners from another network with the comment, 'You have joined us at a very interesting time. Ray Illingworth is just relieving himself at the pavilion end.'

Johnston has even been known to raise eyebrows by simply naming the players. Commentating on the 1976 Oval Test against the West Indies he announced: 'The bowler's Holding, the batsman's Willey.'

Perhaps his most memorable verbal slip was the spoonerism that resulted from an over-zealous attempt to say of one player: 'He's sticking out his bottom – like someone sitting on a shooting stick.'

You don't need to be watching television or listening to the radio to be confronted with statements that are liable to misinterpretation. You need only go out for a walk. In Devon, outside the Barnstaple Health Centre, there is a sign that reads: 'Family Planning – Please use rear entrance.' . . . In Merseyside you will find a large notice that says: 'LIVERPOOL MATERNITY HOSPITAL (Not Accidents)' . . . In a park in Dayton, Ohio, there is a bandstand with seats all around it and a notice that explains: 'The seats in the vicinity of the bandstand are for the use of ladies. Gentlemen should make use of them only after the former are seated.'

The world's leading authority on sexual disasters of the verbal kind is undoubtedly Dan Schuckat, a newspaper proofreader from Brooklyn, New York, who over the past twenty-five years has been collecting printed 'bloomers and bloopers' from newspapers and magazines around the world. Here are some of the gems from his unique collection. First, a few headlines:

MOUNTING PROBLEMS FOR NEWLY-WEDS – *The San Francisco Examiner*
HONEYMOON IF WE CAN FIT IT IN, SAY COUPLE – *Northern Echo*
STRIPPED GIRL – YARD TO PROBE – London *Evening Standard*
TWENTY YEAR FRIENDSHIP ENDS AT THE ALTAR – *Portsmouth Echo*
LOCAL MAN HAS LONGEST HORNS IN TEXAS – *The Denton Record Chronicle*
NEWLY-WEDS AGED 82, HAVE PROBLEM – *The Staten Island Advance*
ARCHDEACON TURNS SOD – *Petersfield Post*

And here are just some of the fascinating items you can pick up from almost any newspaper you care to read – with a filthy mind and a fine-tooth comb:

He said his favourite pastime was standing on a haystack abusing sheep.

New Zealand Times

You really have seen only half the show if you see the Paris imports worn by the mannequins alone. There is almost double the excitement in looking under and inside the clothes.

Women's Wear Daily

New screwing method cuts fatigue and increases productivity.

Engineering Maintenance

The rule was that a girl would not be allowed in the bra without a man.

Exeter Express and Echo

The Tories have been under some pressure to toughen up their party political broadcasts. Mr Heath, Mr MacLeod and Mr Peter Walker accordingly reached for their choppers.

The Guardian

Miss Goldhurst has NO Male Goat this season, and refers all clients to Mr Harris.

Grantham Journal

Wanted: Some additional female technicians at the fast-expanding Charles River Breeding Laboratory. No previous experience necessary.

Massachusetts Chronicle

Home urgently needed for cow. Marriage broken, cannot afford to keep her.

Dairy Farmer

At the annual meeting at Bradwall Village Hall, Mr Tom Bunn presented the various trophies won by members over the year. The Yarwood Trophy for the best male member went to Charles Boffey of Bereton.

Crewe Chronicle

Dan Schuckat's collection of verbal bloomers extends beyond the printed page and the English-speaking world. He also collects the pleasantly ambiguous signs and notices that sometimes appear in foreign hotels and restaurants. Here are four of his favourites:

A notice in the bedroom of a Milan hotel: 'Do not adjust your light hanger. If you wish to have it off the manageress will oblige you.'

A notice in the foyer of a Tokyo hotel: 'Sports jackets may be worn, but no trousers.'

A notice in a Swiss hotel bedroom: 'If you have any desires during the night pray ring for the chambermaid.'

A notice in a café in Dinard: 'Persons are requested not to occupy seats in this café without consummation.'

A few years ago the hazards of international communication were revealed with startling clarity when President Carter made an official visit to Poland. Descending the steps of his aircraft the President was met by 500 leading Poles to whom he addressed what he hoped would be received as fraternal greetings. His words were translated by a State Department interpreter who turned out to have a maverick knowledge of Polish. Innocent errors like the translation of 'When I left the United States' as 'When I abandoned the United States' were soon swamped by more serious gaffes. Apart from telling his hosts, to their ears at least, that their constitution was 'a subject of ridicule', remarks like 'I understand your hopes for the future' came out as 'I know your lust for the future.' The crowning glory came when the President said, 'I have come to learn your opinions and understand your desires for the future,' which was delivered to his audience as, 'I desire to know the Poles carnally.'

Of course, you can speak perfect English and still be misunderstood. The American journalist John Randall confessed recently that when he first came to Britain just after the war he ordered two Bristols when he wanted two glasses of Bristol Cream sherry and thought that 'cobblers' were the right people to repair his shoes.

He was not to know that to the vulgar British 'Bristols' are also breasts and 'cobblers' can be testicles. What was worse for Mr Randall was that he thought a 'fanny' was a backside all over the English-speaking world. It's a backside Stateside, but a female frontside in the British Isles.

This particular piece of Anglo-American ambiguity led to a memorable moment during the filming of *The Taming of the Shrew* in 1966. Franco Zeffirelli, the film's director, asked Richard Burton to grab Elizabeth Taylor by her fanny. As the cameras rolled, Burton did exactly as he thought he had been asked. By all accounts the footage was entertaining, but sadly it ended up on the cutting-room floor.

For some people their very names are sexual disasters. Not everyone is happy to be called Fanny or Roger or Dick. Believe it or not, these are the unlikely and, let's be frank, more than unfortunate names of thirteen real people:

Drew Peacock is a marine biologist in San Diego, California.
Ophelia Ball was a lecturer in Seattle, Washington.
Gay Hooker is a waitress in La Crosse, Wisconsin.
Ivor Krutch is a taxi driver in Toronto, Ontario.

Violet Organ was a distinguished art historian and biographer.

Fanny Finger is alive and well and living in New York City.

Private Parts served in the US Army.

In the United States in 1963 a Mr Cock married a Miss Prick.

Hyman Peckeroff is a New York taxi driver.

Miss Friendly Ley was a resident of Mission Hills, California.

Joy Bang was a Broadway actress.

Mustafa Kunt served as Turkish Military Attaché in Moscow.

Miss Pensive Cocke worked as a secretary in the US Army Air Corps.

In August 1979 a Welsh court fined David Jeremy, a carpenter from Merthyr Tydfil, £18 for trying to obtain a passport under the name of Nassa Ocovish.

In giving evidence Jeremy told the court: 'I fell in love with Miss Jane Plum at first sight. When she told me that she was interested in foreigners I told her that I was the son of a Puerto Rican uranium miner named Nassa Ocovish – a name that just came into my mind. For two years she has known me as Nassa. Whenever we went out I had to pick places where I was unknown. But there were always people around who used to shout "Hello Dave" and things like that. Finally I decided to get a document that would prove who I was, but it was my undoing.'

Any number of entertainers have changed their names. Marti Caine was once Lynda Crapper. Jane Wyman was Sarah Jane Fulks. Diana Dors was Diana Fluck.

Legend has it that soon after she had changed her name and set off on the high road to stardom, Miss Dors was invited back to her home town to open a garden fête. Apparently the Vicar who was to introduce her from the platform was eager to use her real name but anxious lest he make an unfortunate slip of the tongue. When the time came he concentrated hard, so determined was he not to omit the all-important L from the surname. 'Ladies and Gentlemen,' he declared, 'I am going to ask you to welcome a very special person here this afternoon. She is known to the world as Diana Dors. She is better known to us of course as plain Diana Clunt.'

The more important the occasion the more unfortunate the verbal blunder.

Many years ago the late, great Queen Mary was being shown round the newly opened Pleasure Gardens at Battersea in London. The old Queen was famous for her terrifying toques, her ramrod back, her imperious manner, and her stern sense of propriety, so that from the start of the tour the poor director of the Pleasure Gardens was a bundle of nerves. Naturally, he was determined not to put a foot wrong and as the hour-long visit proceeded he did his very best to keep his royal guest informed and, he hoped, modestly entertained.

The last stop on the tour was the new boating lake, in many ways the most important and attractive feature of the gardens. The director was much relieved to have reached the last lap unscathed and allowed himself to relax a little. 'This, Ma'am,' he explained to Her Majesty, 'is our special boating lake where the people can come and enjoy themselves with their cunts and panoes.'

There was a deathly hush as the Royal entourage drew breath and, after an apparently never-ending pause, Queen Mary turned to the hapless director who stood scarlet before her. 'And tell me,' she asked with interest, 'what *exactly* is a panoe?'

You can always trust a true Queen to get you off the hook when you are faced with disaster.

John Aubrey, in his outrageous *Brief Lives*, tells the glorious story of a fart in high places. It concerns Elizabeth I and one of her courtiers, Edward de Vere, 17th Earl of Oxford.

'The Earl of Oxford, making of his low obeisance to Queen Elizabeth, happened to let a fart, at which he was so abashed and ashamed that he went to Travell, seven years. On his return the Queen welcomed him home, and said "My Lord, I had forgott the fart."'

YOU GOTTA HAVE STYLE

'Women are a problem, but if you haven't already guessed, they're the kind of problem I enjoy wrestling with.'

Warren Beatty

'I'm not a gentleman's gentleman, miss, I'm a cad's cad.'

'I am twenty-nine, single; I neither drink nor smoke,' wrote a reader to *Health For All*. 'I do not seem to be able to overcome the sex impulse. Is this due to catarrh, and will a diet of vegetables and salads help to abate it?'

Let's face it, nobody is immune from sexual disaster, but some of us are better equipped to cope than others. Here, to inspire and assist you, is a parting sampling of stories about a variety of real people who have been confronted with a wide range of sexual humiliation, harassment and havoc and yet have managed to survive simply because they had what it takes – and that's style.

Frau Magda Friedrich of Munich has style. With her twenty-seventh wedding anniversary approaching and her husband's passion ebbing, Frau Friedrich splashed out on a bright pink see-through nightdress designed to make this an anniversary to remember.

Her investment paid off. Frau Friedrich was overjoyed, and, having decided that it was the colour of her nightdress rather than its style that had fired the dormant embers of Herr Friedrich's lust, she resolved to help her marriage still further by extending her pink wardrobe. She went shopping and kitted herself out with a two-piece pink suit, with pink gloves, pink hat and pink handbag to match. To go with the clothes, of course, she bought a whole range of livid pink make-up.

Apparently, Herr Friedrich, a dentist by profession, expressed no opinion on the subject of his wife's pink appearance, but when she decided to transform her home as well as herself the poor man began to protest. Pink wallpaper, pink carpets, pink table linen, pink towels, curtains, chairs, electric light bulbs, even a permanent pink tint to the colour television set, all followed in a nauseous wave. Then Frau Friedrich went too far and dyed her husband's dental chair Husk Blush Winter Poppy.

Herr Friedrich went to his lawyer, but Frau Friedrich was unrepentant. 'I am just mad about the colour. I'm going to be divorced in pink.'

Twenty-three-year-old Terri Bodek of Buffalo, New York, is another fashion-conscious wife who decided to get divorced in style. Early in 1984 Mrs Bodek fell in love with pop star Boy George. Now she dresses like him and is divorcing Mr Bodek in order to travel the world in the wake of her idol. Boy George has not yet spoken to Mrs Bodek, but at a concert in Buffalo she managed to secure a front seat and handed him a rose. Apparently the singer took it and smiled. 'It's a start,' said Mrs Bodek.

People have varying attitudes to divorce. After seventeen years of marriage, Mrs Daisy Enford, a mother of three, realized she couldn't put up with her husband's indifference any longer.

On the day she decided to make the break she called to him as he worked in his vegetable patch, 'I am getting a divorce.'

'If I don't get these tomato plants in soon they will die,' he replied.

It takes all sorts to make a world. Some get divorced in style. Some get married in style.

When twenty-nine-year-old Albert Demerra married twenty-three-year-old Anita Falk in New York in 1980 the guests were treated to slices of a most original wedding cake: it was modelled from life and depicted the bride and groom naked and making love.

Traditionally, at least, before the marriage comes the proposal. And inevitably there are ways and ways of proposing...

Clarice Rayner, of Fredericksburg, Virginia, told the court hearing her divorce case that her husband had proposed to her 'on the john'. 'I knew then that it was a mistake to marry him, but he looked so lost sitting there I hadn't the heart to say no.'

Joanna Simmonds of Leeds in Yorkshire revealed in court that her husband had proposed to her while smoking a pipe. 'He thought it made him look manly. I realize now it was just a cover for his homosexual tendencies.'

Sally Ann Romera, of Queens, New York, told the judge hearing her divorce suit that her husband had proposed to her on the night they first met. 'We were standing inside his dad's garage at the time making love. I said Yes because I was frightened he'd beat me up if I didn't.'

In fact, it is possible to turn a man down with dignity and style. Women have been doing it for centuries. Here is how a lady handled an unwelcome written proposal back in 1834:

After the decided disapprobation I have constantly evinced to your attentions, I was rather surprised at receiving an offer of marriage from you.

I am sorry that you have thus placed me under the disagreeable necessity of speaking on a subject so repugnant to my feelings; but candour and truth compel me to return an instant and positive negative to your proposal.

I trust, therefore, you will no longer persist in disturbing, by such unavailing efforts, the peace of sir, your obedient servant...

Of course, even if you accept a proposal in haste you can always decide to marry at leisure. Adriana Martinez and Octavio Guillen were both aged eighty-two when eventually they married in Mexico in 1969. They had been engaged for just over sixty-seven years.

The Casanova of Carlisle, Pennsylvania, is a suave sixty-year-old called Paul Crafton who richly deserves the title of the world's most ardent lover, even though he's not the marrying kind.

Until January 1984 Mr Crafton managed to carry on simultaneous affairs with fifty-three different women. Unfortunately, he also adopted thirty-three different aliases, falsely obtained ninety-six different credit cards, and fraudulently opened over two hundred different bank accounts. He may be in prison now, but no one can deny that, in his own way, Paul Crafton had style – and energy.

The same could be said of Joyce McKinney. 'For the love of Kirk, I would have skied down Everest in the nude with a carnation up my nose', was the extravagant claim she made in court in the autumn of 1977.

Joyce, busty, blonde and twenty-seven, and her friend, Keith May, were jointly charged with kidnapping a twenty-one-year-old Mormon missionary, her former lover Kirk Anderson. According to the prosecution, Kirk had been forcibly taken from his church in Ewell, Surrey, driven to a hideaway cottage in Devon, chained to a bed for three days, and forced to have sex with the rapacious Joyce.

When her turn came to give evidence Joyce explained to the court that she and Kirk had been lovers and that he feared excommunication from the Mormon Church as a result of having broken his missionary vow of celibacy. In her view he had sex problems, and by tying him to the bed in chains she was merely trying to ease them. She also told the court that before leaving her Kirk had made her pregnant, causing her to have an abortion. The only reason she had kidnapped him on this occasion was in order to become pregnant; that achieved she had been prepared to let him go.

Joyce was sent for trial at the Old Bailey, but she and Keith May jumped bail and, posing as deaf mutes, flew off to the United States where they went into hiding in Atlanta, Georgia, disguised as Red Indians.

The late Lady Veronica McLeod had style. She was the only daughter of a distinguished British General and in the London of the 1890s a celebrated beauty. It was then the heyday of the British Raj and her father had been stationed in India for some years. When she was nineteen she sailed out to visit him and on the crossing fell head over heels in love with a handsome young steward in second class. At the ship's fancy dress ball they managed to dance together all evening and then slipped away to Veronica's cabin where they spent a blissful night.

The following morning the young steward had to be up long before his lady-love in order to serve breakfast to his passengers. When he caught up with Lady Veronica later in the day she reproved him icily for his familiarity. 'In the circles in which I move,' she explained, 'sleeping with a woman does not constitute an introduction.'

Lady Veronica McLeod had a wonderful way with words. Some people do. After major eye surgery to restore his sight, Alexander Robinson had his dressings removed for

the first time in the presence of his wife and set their marriage on a new footing with his first words to her: 'Boy, you
sure have got fat in four years.'

When handling a sexual disaster you need to keep your
nerve. It isn't always easy.

Recently a man with three previous convictions for indecent exposure was arrested on a fourth count when he
dropped his trousers and bared his backside to a group of
girls. When he was asked by the magistrates to explain his
action he admitted guilt adding, 'It was a stupid compromise.'

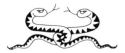

When disaster befalls them, those with an instinctive sense
of style always have the perfect excuse effortlessly at hand.

In 1983 an Irishman was arrested when he was seen by
police walking naked down a street in Solihull. Asked to
explain himself, the man said he was taking part in some
filming for the *Game For A Laugh* television show. Asked to
explain where the film cameras were, the man said they
were hidden in the offices of the National Westminster
Bank further down the street. Asked to explain his apparent
state of arousal, the man said he had never appeared on
television before and the excitement of the occasion had got
the better of him.

Despite the by-laws banning nudity, Lorient Beach in
Brittany has long been a popular *rendez-vous* for nature
lovers. During one of their periodic raids the police arrested

one naked man who protested that he was by no means a nudist. He was, he maintained, a member of 'Decency', an anti-nudist group, and had been sent to the beach merely as a spy.

Unfortunately for the man in question, the police had been observing his behaviour for some while and had watched him on the beach 'romping with four bare-breasted young ladies'. 'I was asking them the way off the beach,' he explained with commendable *sang-froid*.

Two young actors, on a tour of the North of England, were just managing to make ends meet by staying at theatrical digs where the legendary warm-hearted generosity of the landladies made it possible for them to survive quite comfortably on their meagre wages. At one particular establishment in Manchester the two young men had hopes that their comely landlady's good nature might extend to the comforts of bed as well as board. However the end of the week came around without any joy in that direction and it seemed they had been mistaken. The lady had proved friendly, but disappointingly respectable.

After the final performance on Saturday one of them decided to stay on at the theatre for a few drinks with the rest of the company. His friend opted for an early night in anticipation of the rigours of Crewe station the following day. Arriving back at the digs, ravenously hungry, having missed out on the late supper which usually awaited them immediately after the show, the first actor tiptoed stealthily to the kitchen with the intention of making himself a large cheese sandwich. As he snapped on the light he found himself confronted by the sight of his friend, enthusiastically humping their hostess on the kitchen table. Absorbed in what he was doing the young man did not immediately notice the intrusion, but the landlady most definitely did and was consequently covered in confusion. Battling gamely to recover her propriety, though pinned to the table, she turned her head and said in her best social voice, 'Oh, Mr Robinson, you must think me a terrible flirt.'

A Sydney policewoman who was approached for prostitution by a young man whom she promptly arrested was told that he and a friend were 'both keen sociology students finishing an all-Australia survey of sex-tariffs'.

A twenty-three-year-old electrician caught having a shower with the young swimming pool attendant at the Holiday Inn in Birmingham told the Assistant Manager who found them, 'There's nothing to worry about. I'm her brother.'

A London man apprehended drilling a hole in the partition between male and female lavatories told police: 'I had just bought a Bumper Tool outfit and could not wait until I got home to try it.'

A nineteen-year-old Tennessee housewife appeared before a grand jury and admitted having sex with some 5,000 assorted policemen in and around her home in Memphis. She asked that her behaviour be excused on the grounds that her promiscuity was not of her own making. 'I am bringing an action for $1,000,000 against a health spa,' she informed the court. 'There, trapped for ninety minutes in the sauna, I changed from a devout Catholic housewife into a raving nymphomaniac.'

The unseen pressures of life in the sex industry were graphically brought home by a blue-movie star and owner of a chain of 'adult' shops after her arrest for shoplifting. 'I just did not know what I was doing,' she told reporters. 'It has been nothing but work, work, work for the last two years. In over thirty sex films I have performed more than 2,000 erotico-gymnastic acts. You can see that I am dazed by it all because the goods for which I forgot to pay were all dog foods and I poisoned my alsatian Casanova by mistake last week.'

A London man admitted in court that he had had sexual intercourse with a thirteen-year-old girl but said he had stopped seeing her when he found out how old she really was. Prosecuting counsel asked sceptically if he cared 'tuppence' whether or not the girl had reached the age of consent. 'Yes, I'm very fussy,' answered the accused indignantly. 'I'm a respectable married man.'

A company director who appeared before magistrates in Birmingham on a charge of causing a breach of the peace was asked to account for his unusual sense of dress. His explanation was quite straightforward: 'It relaxes me to wear a black bra under a see-through blouse, panty-hose, silver-plated heels and false eyelashes,' he said. 'Such things are worn every day by the London hippy jet-set men. I feel I am being discriminated against on grounds of age.'

The court was told that the defendant was eighty-four.

In October 1979 the *Australian Express* reported the distressing mail-order blunder in which a ninety-one-year-old lady assistant to the verger of Muroorie, Queensland received a nine-inch dildo wrapped in a copy of *Sexual Intercourse – The Full Facts* in place of the luminous statue of the Virgin Mary which she had ordered.

The dispatch manager for the company, Ave Enterprises, expressed his company's regret, saying: 'This is our biggest booboo yet. We deal in sex aids and religious trinkets. We are serious people. We apologise. I am the secretary of the local *Vegetarians Against The Nazis Group*.'

A Liverpool man who was woken early one morning by a loud crash in his kitchen rushed down to see what had happened and found a naked man sitting on the floor beneath a large hole in the roof; he called the police. When they arrived the intruder introduced himself as a brother in uniform. 'After night duty I went to a party,' he told his fellow policemen. 'When I got home I undressed and went to the lavatory. It's outside. I was just about to enter my convenience when three men grabbed me, picked me up, and hurled me through the air on to Mr Shield's roof. Naturally I fell through. There is no truth in the suggestion that I was eavesdropping.'

The case went to court where the officer's counsel pleaded that, as a policeman, he 'could have told the court any number of credible stories. However, he always tells this one.'

Several years ago a group of railway workers in Hungary received a welcome break from routine when they sighted a man, naked from the waist down, jumping from a burning train and racing off down the track. They gave chase and eventually caught up with him. Assuming he was an escaped lunatic they took him to the nearest asylum where he was clapped into a strait jacket. It took three days for him to convince doctors that he was not insane but the victim of a bizarre chain of circumstances.

The man, a keen amateur bee-keeper, had been travelling to Budapest with a consignment of bees safely confined in milk bottles sealed with brown paper.

Unfortunately the bees had taken strong exception to their cramped quarters and by half-way through the journey a large number of them had wriggled free and were crawling up the man's legs. Naturally the ladies travelling in the same compartment had been sympathetic to his plight and obligingly left while he took off his trousers to sort out the problem. At the moment of removal a passing express train had hurtled by, creating a powerful airstream which whisked the swarming trousers into the corridor and wrapped them round the neck of the ticket inspector. Totally unnerved the bees had lashed out in self-defence and set about the unfortunate official. His immediate reaction was to pull the communication cord, which brought the train to a screeching halt, whereupon it promptly burst into flames. At this point the bee-keeper had been overwhelmed by total panic and fled from the scene of the disaster.

Not all sexual disasters can be explained away with equal ease. Some have a terrible finality about them.

In 1899 Felix Fauré had been President of France for four years when he succumbed to the temptations of a specially designed 'sex chair'. The experience proved too much for the fifty-eight-year-old statesman who died of a heart attack while he and his mistress were still 'seated'.

Betty Grant worked for a firm of wholesale chemists where she caught the amorous eye of one of her colleagues. In the hope of furthering their acquaintance he gave her an innocent-looking piece of chocolate-covered coconut ice, which Betty shared with her friend June Malins. Unknown to the girls the coconut ice had been spiked with cantharadin, the chemical found in the medieval aphrodisiac Spanish Fly. Unfortunately the young man was not aware of the fact that cantharadin is also a lethal poison. Within twenty-four hours he was more of a lady-killer than he bargained for.

As a rule sex won't kill you, but there are moments when disaster strikes and you might well wish you were dead...

Returning from a shopping expedition one day a woman from Anchorage, Alaska found her husband working underneath his car. His legs were sticking out and as she passed him his wife reached down and gave a playful squeeze to the 'family jewel box' before going inside. There to her horror was her husband cleaning some part of the braking system in the kitchen. Meanwhile their neighbour was walking groggily to the door with a cut in his forehead that needed four stitches.

The French journalist and broadcaster Jacques Ferrand tells what he claims to be the true story of a young English couple on their way to a camping holiday in the south of France.

Thrilled at the thought of an uninterrupted fortnight together under canvas and away from the prying eyes of friends and family, the young lovers' thoughts had been turning more and more to one topic ever since they had embarked on the ferry at Dover. By the time they were driving through Paris both were in a frenzy of passion and unable to wait any longer to do something about it. They stopped in the Bois de Boulogne and, space being somewhat restricted in their car, got out and clambered underneath in order to enjoy themselves without being discomfited by the slight drizzle which was falling.

The next thing the young man became aware of was the face of a French policeman uncomfortably close to his, and a voice reminiscent of Inspector Clouseau saying, 'What are you doing zer?' Thinking (metaphorically) on his feet the young man replied, 'Mending the car.' 'M'sieu,' responded the other, 'let me geev you three raisons why you are *not* mending your car! *Vone*, you are ze wrong way up. *Two*, zer are fifteen Frenchmen standing round you shouting "*Vive le sport!*" And *three*, someone 'as stolen your car.'

'Marriage,' said Ambrose Bierce, 'is a community consisting of a master, a mistress and two slaves – making two in all.' Eddie Fisher and Zsa Zsa Gabor are equally cynical authorities on the subject. Says Mr Fisher: 'Women would be the most enchanting creatures in the world if in falling into their arms one didn't fall into their hands.' Says Miss Gabor: 'A man in love is incomplete until he is married. Then he's finished.'

The best that can be said for marriage is that it is at least full of surprises...

A Canberra woman whose husband was always too slow off the mark in bed decided that a sudden shock might get his blood moving and speed things up. She hid in the bedroom when he came home from work and then jumped out at him with a terrifying shriek. In some respects her plan worked perfectly. The poor man was scared out of his wits. He dashed for the door in a blind panic, tripped over a chair, tumbled down the stairs and ended up in bed – but in hospital.

In England in the Bad Old Days it required an Act of Parliament to obtain a divorce and naturally the only people able to afford to end their marriages in this way were the well-to-do. There was one notable exception to the rule – the Town Clerk of a council in the Midlands.

The Town Clerk had been married for many years, few of which had been remotely enjoyable. He knew that divorce through the normal channels was financially impossible and had resigned himself to enduring a miserable home-life. Then a glimmer of light appeared, not at the end of a tunnel, but at the end of a drain-pipe.

The town council was proposing to install a municipal water and sewage system which required its own Waterworks Bill. The Town Clerk had the responsibility for drafting this before it was sent to Parliament and he took the liberty of inserting a personal note in Clause 64.

The bill passed through all its stages and received the royal assent without anyone questioning the entry hidden among details of sewage beds, effluent treatment, pumping stations and water pressures – the one that read 'and the Town Clerk's marriage is hereby dissolved'.

To his wife's intense annoyance the Town Clerk won his freedom without losing a penny.

If you are unlucky in love it is sometimes comforting to be able to do something about it.

A British television director who was unfortunate enough to need to be treated at a VD clinic turned the experience to his advantage by naming as contacts every girl who had ever spurned his advances.

Revenge is sweet.

There is a telling (though possibly apocryphal) story of a Jewish widow returning from her husband's funeral with her best friend. The two elderly ladies decided to have supper together, and in the kitchen the widow began to prepare the meal. She put the frying pan on the stove, threw in a knob of butter, chopped up an onion and then, from her handbag, produced a small paper parcel which she proceeded to unwrap.

'A chippolata,' shrieked her friend, 'I'm not eating a chippolata!'

'It's not a chippolata,' said the widow. 'It's Hymie's schmuck. And it's not for you,' she added, tossing it lightly into the frying pan. 'It's for me. For thirty-six years I ate it his way. Tonight I eat it my way!'

A married airline pilot and his mistress, a young stewardess who worked for the same carrier, set themselves up in a flat in London and lived there in secrecy for a year. Then the pilot grew bored with the relationship and gave his girl-friend her marching orders. She asked to have a few days in which to move out and, since he was on the point of leaving for a spell abroad, the pilot readily agreed.

When he got back to London a fortnight later the girl had gone. The flat was clean and tidy. The only thing the pilot noticed was the telephone receiver left off the hook. He picked it up to replace it and heard an American voice telling him the time – every ten seconds. His girlfriend had dialled the speaking clock in Chicago before leaving and the pilot's next quarterly bill showed a charge of just over £1,200.

A penniless New York actor had the misfortune to fall helplessly in love with the daughter of a leading Wall Street broker. She fell for him too, but her parents hoped for better things and sent her away to relatives in Bermuda until the affair blew over. The parents' wishes proved more powerful than their daughter's passion and it wasn't long before the young actor received a letter from the girl telling him that she had decided to marry the son of a wealthy New York banker. The actor was devastated. Even the offer of a part on Broadway did little to lighten his misery.

A day or two before the wedding was due to take place in St Patrick's Cathedral the jilted actor was pouring out his heart to one of the cast of his new show when she suggested a stylish form of revenge.

On the wedding day the actor lurked at the back of the crowd waiting to see the happy couple leave the cathedral after the service. As the beaming bride and groom paused for the cameras on the steps of St Patrick's a stunningly attractive girl pushed her way forward, threw her arms around the neck of the astonished bridegroom and kissed him passionately on the lips. 'Darling, you may forget,' she declared, 'but I never will. Our years together will live with me forever!'

Following a last desperate embrace, the mysterious young lady left the stunned newly-weds to fight it out as she slipped back into the crowd and joined her fellow actor for the lunch she'd been promised as her reward.

After his marriage to the columnist Ilka Chase ended in divorce, Louis Calhern married Julia Hoyt. Some time later Miss Chase was sorting through a trunk when she came across a box of handsome, engraved cards printed simply with the name 'Mrs Louis Calhern'. Carefully she wrapped them up and sent them to her successor, with a note: 'Dear Julia, I hope these reach you in time.'

'Don't doubt, Miss Bannister, that your fate will be
fully reported in *The Times*.'